Praise for
Find Your Brave

"If you've lost the confidence and strength to endure the storms in your life, *Find Your Brave* is the empowering message your heart needs. With biblical wisdom and personal understanding, Holly will show you what it looks like to fight back against life's disappointments in the only way that works—with the Lord's help. I love this resource."

—LYSA TERKEURST, *New York Times* best-selling author
and president of Proverbs 31 Ministries

"Holly Wagner mixes raw honesty and real wisdom as she helps us navigate the storms that come our way. As you turn the pages of *Find Your Brave,* not only will you learn and be inspired, but at times you will seriously laugh out loud. This book has the potential to be a game changer in the way we respond to the challenges we all face. Why not pick up one for friend?"

—CHRISTINE CAINE, founder of A21 and Propel

"I have known and loved Holly for more than twenty years. Her grasp of the Word of God and her ability to bring it to life is magnificent. She personally has navigated unchartered waters on a number of occasions and always comes through with testimony to the goodness and grace of God. *Find Your Brave* will inspire courage in your own walk."

—BOBBIE HOUSTON, Hillsong Church, author of *The Sisterhood*

"I've always loved the insightful, practical, loving, and loyal way Holly approaches life. In this book, her honesty, mixed with wisdom coming from personal experiences and biblical teaching, encourages the reader to dig deeper and find your brave when walking through adversity. Holly not only reminds us who we are, but she walks alongside us with great encouragement and more often a sisterly push to keep moving forward!"

—DARLENE ZSCHECH, composer, worship leader, and author
of *Worship Changes Everything*

"Holly Wagner is one of the most dynamic and faith-filled people we know. Her new book, *Find Your Brave,* will equip, encourage, and inspire you to take bold steps of faith and stand strong when life gets tough."

—CRAIG AND AMY GROESCHEL, authors of *From This Day Forward*

"*Find Your Brave* is more than a theory for Holly Wagner. She found her brave as she pioneered a church in Hollywood, journeyed through cancer, and battled with fear. This book positions *you* to forge through trials and come out radiant on the other side."

—LISA BEVERE, Messenger International, author of *Lioness Arising*

"Holly doesn't write about finding your brave from the sidelines; she writes from the heart of the battle. Because she lives out her message daily, she helps us understand that we too can find our brave. Not only that, the journey is exhilarating, and when we do it together, we are stronger."

—SHEILA WALSH, author of *The Longing in Me*

"We know challenges will come to us all; none are exempt. In *Find Your Brave,* Holly masterfully maps the way to finding and sourcing inner strength in those trying times. Her humor sets you at ease while her words stir, inspire, and spur you on to a live a life filled with courage and faith."

—PASTORS JUDAH AND CHELSEA SMITH, lead pastors
of The City Church in Seattle, Washington

"In *Find Your Brave,* Holly Wagner empowers women to stand strong as an example to the world. She reminds us that it is in our strength that we find our purpose, and it is only through God that we find our strength. For any woman who has ever faced fear, this book is a must-read!"

—LISA YOUNG, Fellowship Church, coauthor
of *The Creative Marriage*

"We all face dark and challenging times. In *Find Your Brave,* Holly Wagner will show you how to find the courage to rise up, press through your storm, and triumph on the other side."

—HOLLY FURTICK, wife of Steven Furtick, pastor of Elevation
Church in Charlotte, North Carolina

FIND
YOUR
BRAVE

FIND YOUR BRAVE

Courage to Stand Strong When the Waves Crash In

HOLLY WAGNER

WATERBROOK

All Scripture quotations, unless otherwise indicated, are taken from the Holy Bible, New International Version®, NIV®. Copyright © 1973, 1978, 1984, 2011 by Biblica Inc.® Used by permission. All rights reserved worldwide. Scripture quotations marked (AMP) are taken from the Amplified Bible. Copyright © 2015 by the Lockman Foundation. Used by permission. (www.Lockman.org). Scripture quotations marked (AMPC) are taken from the Amplified Bible Classic Edition. Copyright © 1954, 1958, 1962, 1964, 1965, 1987 by the Lockman Foundation. Used by permission. (www.Lockman.org). Scripture quotations marked (CEV) are taken from the Contemporary English Version. Copyright © 1991, 1992, 1995 by American Bible Society. Used by permission. Scripture quotations marked (ESV) are taken from the ESV® Bible (the Holy Bible, English Standard Version®), copyright © 2001 by Crossway, a publishing ministry of Good News Publishers. Used by permission. All rights reserved. Scripture quotations marked (MSG) are taken from The Message. Copyright © by Eugene H. Peterson 1993, 1994, 1995, 1996, 2000, 2001, 2002. Used by permission of Tyndale House Publishers Inc. Scripture quotations marked (NCV) are taken from the New Century Version®. Copyright © 2005 by Thomas Nelson Inc. Used by permission. All rights reserved. Scripture quotations marked (NKJV) are taken from the New King James Version®. Copyright © 1982 by Thomas Nelson Inc. Used by permission. All rights reserved. Scripture quotations marked (NLT) are taken from the Holy Bible, New Living Translation, copyright © 1996, 2004, 2007 by Tyndale House Foundation. Used by permission of Tyndale House Publishers Inc., Carol Stream, Illinois 60188. All rights reserved.

Italics in Scripture quotations—except The Message version—reflect the author's added emphasis. Where emphasis is added to The Message version, it is indicated with the Scripture reference.

Details in some anecdotes and stories have been changed to protect the identities of the persons involved.

Hardcover ISBN 978-1-60142-879-0
eBook ISBN 978-1-60142-880-6

Copyright © 2016 by Holly Wagner

Cover design by Mark D. Ford

Published in the United States by WaterBrook, an imprint of the Crown Publishing Group, a division of Penguin Random House LLC, New York.

WATERBROOK® and its deer colophon are registered trademarks of Penguin Random House LLC.

Library of Congress Cataloging-in-Publication Data
Names: Wagner, Holly, author.
Title: Find your brave : courage to stand strong when the waves crash in / Holly Wagner.
Description: First Edition. | Colorado Springs, Colorado : WaterBrook Press, 2016. | Includes bibliographical references.
Identifiers: LCCN 2016000204 (print) | LCCN 2016007185 (ebook) | ISBN 9781601428790 (hardcover) | ISBN 9781601428806 (electronic)
Subjects: LCSH: Christian women. | Courage—Religious aspects—Christianity. | Fortitude.
Classification: LCC BV4527 .W2965 2016 (print) | LCC BV4527 (ebook) | DDC 248.8/43—dc23
LC record available at http://lccn.loc.gov/2016000204

Printed in the United States of America
2016—First Edition

10 9 8 7 6 5 4 3 2 1

SPECIAL SALES
Most WaterBrook books are available at special quantity discounts when purchased in bulk by corporations, organizations, and special-interest groups. Custom imprinting or excerpting can also be done to fit special needs. For information, please e-mail specialmarketscms@penguinrandomhouse.com or call 1-800-603-7051.

───

This book is dedicated to you, the reader, as you navigate the real storms of life. I know life can be messy, so thanks for not giving up and for your commitment to honor God as the waves of the storm crash against your life. You are not alone!

───

Contents

Rising in the Darkness

Nothing splendid has ever been achieved
except by those who dared believe that
something inside of them was superior to
circumstance.

—Bruce Barton

And though she be but little, she is fierce.

—William Shakespeare

t felt like a bomb was exploding under my bed. Our house alarm system
was screeching, and I could hear dishes hitting the kitchen's tile floor
and shattering into a million pieces. The whole world seemed to be shaking. The electricity went out, and I could not see my hand in front of my
face.

You may not remember where you were at 4:31 a.m. on January 17,
1994 (other than in bed), but I will never forget. We were experiencing a
massive magnitude 6.7 earthquake in Los Angeles. I had felt small tremors before but nothing close to this. The shaking was terrible, and the
noise was even worse. I have since learned that when an earthquake occurs, the first waves to hit are the primary, seismic waves, which cause

destruction as they hit various objects. The destruction caused is loud. That explained the bomb-like sound.

As the quaking continued, my husband, Philip, yelled that he would get Paris, our two-and-a-half-year-old daughter, and that I should grab our six-year-old son, Jordan. The house was pitch black. I glanced out our window and noticed that our whole neighborhood was dark, so I didn't even have ambient city light to guide me. The earthquake still rumbled as I stumbled across our bedroom to get to the hall. A dresser flew across the room and clipped me in the legs, forcing me to my knees. Now I was crawling to get to my son. Panicked, I barely noticed the shards slicing into my hands and legs from the shattered glass of fallen pictures. But I am a mom, and like most moms, I did whatever was necessary to get to my kids!

When I reached my son's door, I couldn't open it. Something had fallen on the other side and blocked it.

"Jordan?! Jordan, open this door!"

"Mom, I'm all right!" his scared little voice penetrated the door and pierced my heart. Eventually, we got the door open, and I clutched him close while we stood in the doorway, as those of us who live in earthquake zones have been instructed to do.

Philip was holding Paris in her bedroom doorway, and we all braced ourselves as the first aftershock hit. It was just a little less intense than the initial jolt, but still frightening. Philip realized that we needed to get out of the house, so we grabbed a blanket and made our way downstairs and out to the front lawn. (It was winter, which in Los Angeles can be tough— sixty degrees or so. Don't hate.) Somebody remembered to get the dog, and we all huddled under the blanket. The most important people—and animal—in the world to me were under that blanket on the lawn.

A few houses near us exploded when their gas lines burst. We were afraid and anxious as burning embers flew over our heads.

Finally the sun began to make its way over the horizon, and we could see the devastation around us. Blood oozed down my leg where the dresser had hit me—I hadn't noticed the injury until that point. I carry the scars still.

I entered our house and was stunned to see the chaos. Every wall was cracked, the chandelier had swung so hard it had broken a wall, the television and computer had been thrown across the room, all the plates and glasses were crushed into thousands of tiny pieces, and the kitchen appliances were no longer in the kitchen. In the light of day, the scene was shocking. The damage came to around seventy thousand dollars. At that moment, I wasn't sure what to do next. I just knew that I wanted our nightmare experience to end. Right away.

You may never face an earthquake like the one I experienced. I certainly hope not! But I've found it isn't only the literal earthquakes that can tear us up. Figurative earthquakes can rock our lives with chaos and fear. And the aftershocks can feel just as devastating.

At some point, the unfortunate reality is that we all *will* face some kind of earthquake, our own dark, scary challenge. The decisions we make during those difficult times are crucial; they determine whether or not we'll make it through with our faith, relationships, and sanity intact. In the midst of our earthquake, Philip and I made some good decisions that led our family to safety, and we almost made some that I believe could have brought more damage (more about those later).

The Bible tells us not to think it strange when a "fiery ordeal" comes our way.[1] Just so ya know, I always think it is strange. But perhaps we need to make the decision not to take personally every challenge we face. Some trials might be of our making—our own bad choices, which we'll discuss later—but plenty occur simply because we live on earth. God is not mad at you or me, and He is not punishing us. Challenges come to the good and the bad, to the just and the unjust . . . they come to us all. They are not those elective courses we get to choose in college, but rather they are part of the core curriculum of life.

WE NEED THOSE CHALLENGES?

We face troubles of all kinds in our world, our country, our cities, our friendships, our families, and within our own hearts. Jesus promised us that in this world we would have trials, distress, and frustration—*but* that we should be at peace, because He has defeated the world for us and shown us how to overcome it as well.[2]

When my daughter, Paris, was in middle school, we had to participate in the school's science fair. The teacher's instructions stated that parents were not supposed to help. I was happy about those directions; I had already graduated from middle school and felt no desire to do another science project. Paris was interested in horses, so she chose to build a papier-mâché horse, or what vaguely resembled a horse, which leaned significantly to the left. I helped her carry her project to the fair and was interested in seeing all the other sixth-grade projects. After we set up Paris's horse display, I looked around the room. I saw some amazing projects, including a giant set of lungs that breathed and a map of the United States that lit up according to how much power each city used. I looked back at Paris's unique leaning horse and quickly realized that either some parents cheated or we had somehow ended up at a university science fair!

After I reassured Paris that her project was interesting, I began to walk around the room, mainly to give myself time to forgive all those cheater parents. As I perused the submissions, I encountered the most amazing project: a miniature re-creation of the Biosphere 2, which I am *so sure* was built by a sixth grader. But I'm not bitter.

In 1991, eight scientists lived for two years in an artificial environment in Oracle, Arizona, called Biosphere 2. (How they did that without a Starbucks is beyond me!) Inside the three-acre closed system was a small ocean, a rain forest, a desert, and a savannah grassland. The scientists produced every kind of weather pattern except wind. Eventually the lack of wind caused the tree trunks to grow weak and bend over. It is the pressure of wind that strengthens tree trunks and allows them to hold up their own weight.

As I stared at that sixth-grader's project and thought about the lessons from the Biosphere 2, I realized something important about life. Like it or not, we have to admit that weathering storms builds our strength.

So as much as I hate challenges, I think we need them. Proverbs 31 tells us why. At first glance that chapter in the Bible sounds a bit annoying. It was written as a poem perhaps for men in Israel to memorize and recite as a tribute to women. While not necessarily a job description, many of the verses paint the picture of this seemingly perfect woman. Who could live up to her? Often she is called the "virtuous woman," which sounds like someone who is quiet and does a lot of knitting. (No offense, if you are a knitter.) I am not really good at either of those. I would have been happy for Proverbs to end with chapter 30. Really. However, about twenty years ago, I began the journey of discovering just who a daughter of the King is designed to be, and I had an inkling that understanding Proverbs 31 was going to be essential—not only to my faith but also to help me figure out how to handle challenges that come my way. As I studied, I learned that the word *virtuous* is the Hebrew word *chayil* and has to do with might, strength, and valor. It actually means a "force on the earth."[3]

Wow. We are designed to be a force on the earth. I like that.

WE MUST RISE!

At first I was rather put off by Proverbs 31:15, the verse that challenges us to rise "while it is yet night."[4] What? I don't think so. I sleep while it is yet night. The truth is, however, that verse has less to do with the time of day we get up and everything to do with being women who *rise up* when earthquakes and chaos and heartbreak and calamity abound. In the darkest hour, she rises.

And on a more personal level, perhaps your world is shaking. Maybe cancer has struck your family, or a loved one is addicted to drugs or alcohol, or perhaps divorce has torn apart your home. At times it seems, if for no other reason than the size of the global population, that there has never been more pain, more disease, more famine, and more heartbreak on the planet than now, and yet God has trusted you and me with this moment in history! We are to be a force for good on the earth. *Chayil.* When everything around us is in the midst of chaos, when our own world is quaking, we are to be the *she* who rises.

She does not wilt; she does not complain; she does not blame. She finds her brave and she rises. She actually grows stronger in the midst of dark times when it seems as if the whole world is trembling. God is looking for a company of women who will find their brave and rise in the midst of any and every challenge—and then be a force for good to help others find their brave.

Throughout the Bible we read about women who rose out of a dark situation to bring strength. In the dark days of disorder and confusion during the time of the Judges, when Israel vacillated in its worship of God, a woman named Deborah rose like a mother in Israel. God used her to lead the Israelites to freedom.[5] She found her brave, and she rose to the challenge.

In a terrifying moment, when her people were threatened with genocide, Queen Esther risked her own life to rescue them, and a nation of people was saved.[6] Esther found her brave in dark times and rose to the challenge.

We do not have to remain stuck in our trials! We grow through them, and as daughters of the King, we can rise in the midst of dark, shaking moments. But how?

PAUL KNEW ABOUT TROUBLE

How can we find our brave and rise to the challenges we face? Well, there's another person in the Bible who has some great advice to share.

The apostle Paul intimately understood dark times. In his case, he didn't suffer through an earthquake—it was a storm.

Paul had angered Jewish leaders by preaching the gospel, so they convinced the Roman soldiers that Paul was a troublemaker and had him thrown in jail in Caesarea. Although he was never officially convicted, Paul remained in prison. When he discovered he was going to be beaten, he appealed to Caesar to hear his case (because he was also a Roman citizen). So the soldiers loaded him on a ship headed for Rome. From the beginning of the sea voyage, the winds blew against the boat, and it made slow progress along the coast.

The ship was having difficulty because it left port during a dangerous time for sailing; the winds were already unpredictable. The sailing season was deemed dangerous from mid-September to mid-November, and the waterways closed for travel until February, a period of about three months. It appears that Paul's journey took place in roughly mid-October.[7]

Paul warned the crew that trouble lay ahead. But Julius, the Roman centurion in charge of the prisoners, chose to pay more attention to the ship's captain, who was determined to make his destination during this dangerous season. What started as gentle breezes quickly turned into hurricane-force winds, and the journey of navigating through a storm began. (I feel seasick just thinking about it.)

Acts 27 records his adventure, and it offers encouragement to those of us who are on the journey to find our brave in the midst of a storm. Just like Paul, you and I live in trying times. Every day we need to make decisions that produce the future we want. It is the same when we are in a storm. We must make choices, however hard they might be in the moment, that will get us through to the calm other side—or in Paul's case, to shore in one piece! We don't want to make choices that merely create another storm.

That's why I've written this book. You and I are going to face and struggle through storms. You may be in one right now. While it's never fun, and often it's just really hard, it is possible to survive and grow stronger through it, and because of it, to come out as an overcomer. In the following pages, we will explore how to do that.

But as we will learn, we don't just find our brave and survive the storms for ourselves. God designed us to live in community so that our experiences can help others. People all around us are looking for help as they navigate challenges, and we can demonstrate a victorious way of living, even in challenging times. God gets the glory because it is at our weakest that His strength is revealed in us. After all, Jesus lived in and spoke to storms, and He never allowed them to interfere with His destiny. The same is true for Paul. The same can be true for you and me.

Throughout this book, we will look at some specific things Paul did to survive his storm, and these are the same things we must do to make it through our wind and waves. Not to spoil the ending of the storm story, but Paul and all the people on board survived. The ship carrying them was destroyed, but thanks in large part to Paul's wisdom and decisive actions, he and his shipmates reached their shore. So can you.

As believers, our ultimate shore is heaven, where we will hear Jesus say, "Well done." But throughout life, every storm, whether it involves a relationship, a job, or our health, offers the opportunity not only for survival but also for triumph.

I wrote this book because I want to see you fulfill your individual, God-designed purpose to be brave. That purpose, that bravery, that ability to rise as the Proverbs 31 woman did, will not be handed to us like a participation trophy at a Little League baseball game. We will have to work for it. Remember, we never camp out in the storm; rather, we forge through it and rise as virtuous women—stronger and more secure in our faith, relationships, *and* sanity.

Are you ready to find *your* brave? Then let's get started.

2

Brace Yourself

Truth is powerful and it prevails.

—Sojourner Truth

Two are better than one.

—Ecclesiastes 4:9

I was crossing a small part of my elementary school's athletic field by hanging on to a rope stretched between two poles, twelve feet above the ground. I wasn't trying to be Wonder Woman; I was merely part of a PE class. Hand over hand, I made my way, dangling above the ground. I was doing just fine when suddenly my hands slipped and I fell. *Snap!* There went the bone in my wrist.

I was in pain, but I was more embarrassed that I hadn't made it across the field as the boys had. I was still at the age where I was trying to prove that anything a boy could do, I could do too! A teacher called my mom, who rushed me to the doctor's office, where I got a cast put on my arm.

You may have broken a bone at some point in your life, or maybe your children have. So you are familiar with the fact that the cast holds the reset bone in place in order for it to heal correctly. The cast acts as a brace, a support mechanism, so that the bone can regain its strength.

Without the cast, the patient would suffer a lot of pain and have no guarantee that the bone would heal straight.

Just as a broken arm needs a cast, we too need support mechanisms in order to make it through our difficult times.

FRAP THOSE SUPPORT LINES!

When Paul's ship encountered that incredibly severe storm, the winds and waves threatened to rip the boat apart, so the crew had to act fast.

The sailors wrapped ropes around the ship to hold it together (CEV). They used support lines [for frapping] to undergird and brace the ship's hull (AMP).

—Acts 27:17

In order to save the ship, they had to brace it, so they put ropes under the vessel to hold it together. During that time period, sailors tied cables or strong ropes around a vessel to keep the planks from breaking and leaking. In nautical terms, this passing of ropes in order to support and strengthen is called "frapping." Can you imagine how frightening it must have been for the sailor who had to take the rope, jump into the stormy sea, swim under the ship, emerge on the other side with the rope, tie it down, and then do it again?

The sailors knew, though, that if they were going to make it through the storm, they had to brace the ship so that it wouldn't break apart in the rough seas. It is the same for you and me. If we are going to survive our life storms, whether it is in marriage (and if you have been married longer than six minutes, you have encountered a storm . . . or two . . . or ten), health, career, parenting, or finances, we need to put support mechanisms in place in order to make it safely to shore—which is always the goal!

BRACE 1: FIX YOUR MIND ON THE TRUTH ABOUT GOD

In those weeks after the earthquake of 1994, we experienced thousands of aftershocks. Basically, our earth was never still. I hated it. Every time the ground shook, so did I. I wondered if another quake was coming that would finally cause Southern California to float off into the Pacific Ocean. The jokes about Arizona becoming beachfront property weren't so funny anymore. I was truly afraid, and I realized that I needed to fight the fear if I was going to make it. I couldn't change what the earth was doing, but I could change my perspective.

In the New Testament we are challenged to brace up our minds. Essentially we're told to "think straight."[1] When going through any major life upheaval, we must take control of our thoughts. This first support mechanism helps us declare the truth and set straight our thinking. Our thoughts will ultimately determine our actions, and often our thoughts can lead down a path we don't want to walk. We can't always control the first thought that rushes through our minds, but we can control the second and we can control what we dwell on.

If we are going to reach the shore safely, if we are going to successfully navigate whatever challenge we are facing, we have to manage our thoughts. And honestly, the best place to begin that process is to read the Bible. So to deal with the fear I felt during those aftershocks, I opened my Bible. Psalms is a great place to start. King David, who wrote most of the book, had to deal regularly with fear. He had a number of enemies who wanted him dead, so he had some things to say about it! In Psalm 118, he reminded me that when I turn to God, He will take my worries away. When He is on my side, I don't need to fear.

Over and over, the psalms reiterate this idea. In Psalm 91:9–11, David wrote,

If you say, "The LORD is my refuge,"
     and you make the Most High your dwelling,
no harm will overtake you,
     no disaster will come near your tent.
For he will command his angels concerning you
     to guard you in all your ways.

I said those verses aloud because there were nights I was worried. Every slight earth tremor woke me, and I would sit up in bed, waiting, anxious. To deal with my fear, I quoted those passages out loud so that my mind could hear them! To survive this storm of fear, I had to brace up my mind. I had to control my thoughts.

Faith does come when we hear the Word of God,[2] and sometimes we need to hear it coming from our own mouths. Read a verse in the Bible, then say it out loud.

I know this sounds simple, but this is just the first step. I am not trying to be trite or platitude-y (I'm sure that's not a word), but the truth is, if we don't know His Word, we will not make it out of the storm. Throughout the coming chapters, we'll look at some other steps, including overcoming the past, but for now, start with this brace: read a verse in the Bible, then say it out loud.

Maybe you need peace. We all do, but maybe you are in a situation that is rocking your world, and peace seems far away. How about opening the Bible and reading these verses out loud?

The LORD gives strength to his people [me]; the LORD blesses his people [me] with peace. (Psalm 29:11)

[Jesus said,] "Peace I leave with you; my peace I give you. I do not give to you as the world gives. Do not let your hearts be troubled and do not be afraid." (John 14:27)

Or maybe you are trying to make a decision about your future and the weight of it is pulling you down. How about declaring these verses out loud?

[I will] commit to the LORD whatever [I] do, and he will establish [my] plans. (Proverbs 16:3)

"I know the plans I have for you," declares the LORD, "plans to prosper you and not to harm you, plans to give you hope and a future." (Jeremiah 29:11)

The Bible is truth, and truth has the power to change us. Obviously the facts about a certain situation are important, but facts aren't nearly as crucial as the truth.

For instance, ten years ago I was diagnosed with breast cancer. Invasive Ductal Carcinoma (IDC). I began the journey through a horrific, dark, can't-see-my-hand-in-front-of-my-face kind of storm. There was no getting around the facts of the diagnosis: a cancerous tumor in my right breast. And I had a decision to make: I could let the facts of this diagnosis freak me out, or I could put my hope in the truth. The truth of who God is.

He is good.

He loves me.

He is faithful.

He will never leave me.

I had to choose to place my hope in the truth of His Word. Exodus 15:26 tells me that my God is the One who heals me. Isaiah 38:16 says that He will restore my health. The Gospels are filled with examples of Jesus healing people. Because Jesus said, "If you have seen me, you have seen the Father,"[3] we understand the nature of God is to heal. Not only is He able to heal, He is willing to heal us. I know there are people who are not healed. (I do not live in Fantasyland.) I am just suggesting we have a choice as to where we put our thoughts.

Rather than letting my thoughts dwell on this very real, very scary situation, I chose to focus on the truth of God's character. Some days I was better at it than others, but I *knew* that to make it through this storm, I had to build my life on truth, not just on the facts. And the truth is that we are transformed—or more accurately, our perspective of the facts is transformed—when our minds are renewed, not necessarily when the circumstances change.[4]

Sometimes when we are in the middle of a storm, we want to look for someone to blame—which, honestly, is not helpful. It is okay to be angry and frustrated and sad at our circumstances, but at some point, we have to quit looking for where to place blame and open His Word. Let the truth of His Word be the balm that your soul needs.

You may be experiencing a storm in your health, or maybe someone you love is in the middle of a storm. I am truly sorry. Hold on to the truth. Declare it in the midst of the circumstances; don't let the facts of the doctor's report defeat you. I know that a diagnosis is scary. I know the forceful voices of doctors can be overwhelming and the path forward can be unclear. You are not alone.

Or maybe you just lost your job. Open your Bible, and let the God who loves you with a love beyond compare speak truth to you. His love is real, and where you are now is not the end of your story. Taking control of your thoughts sometimes means choosing to trust even when you don't understand. I know it feels overwhelming right now, but not only will you get through this, you will ultimately help others do the same.

Maybe your storm involves a relationship. The same practical truth applies. Perhaps your engagement just ended. You thought this relationship was headed to the altar and now you find yourself alone again. Your value has not changed, and this is the time to remind yourself that you are worth more than "rubies or pearls,"[5] that the plans God has for you are filled with hope.[6] Let's brace up our lives with the truth—about God, His Word, His strength, and His love for us.

There was a time (okay, actually more than one) when my marriage was in a storm in which I needed to find my brave. Of course, the problem was all Philip's fault! If only he could be more like me. After all, I was practically perfect. The first few years of our marriage were especially trying . . . because I realized that Cinderella lied.

Philip was neither a prince nor charming, and I was ready to throw the slipper at him. We just had too many differences between us, and I wasn't sure we could make it. The scary thing is, I had begun to lose hope.

The facts were overwhelming: too many differences (personalities, backgrounds, and families); I was stubborn; he could be moody and unaffectionate; we weren't happy . . . and the list goes on. No one knows how to push our buttons more than our spouses. Many times I have had to say, "Not my will, but Yours be done, God," because my will would have taken me out the door.

I hope I am not making it sound easy, because it wasn't. I almost gave up.

But now, thirty years later, we have a great life—not without its challenges, but great, nonetheless—with two awesome adult children who love us and love God, a flourishing church, and wonderful friends around the planet. Our marriage didn't get better overnight, but from the moment I started to declare the truth of who God is and His desires for marriage, I saw small signs of improvement. I read books on how to build a marriage. Philip and I attended seminars, and we quit blaming each other for the storms.

Marriages go through seasons, and you and your spouse are not the same people you were when you got married. You have to continually learn and discover the person you married. Maybe your marriage is in the center of a storm. You might have given up on a marriage in the past. I am not here to criticize or judge. Regardless of whether you are working on marriage number one or marriage number twelve, make this the one you finish out life with.

There are real, practical steps we all need to take to build a healthy marriage. And for more of those, read *Love Works,* a book Philip and I wrote together about the sometimes fun, always messy process of dating and marriage. But for now, step one is to speak the truth over your marriage. Just as I did.

> Marriage is precious, of great price, and especially dear. (Hebrews 13:4, my version)

> My husband is deeply in love with me; he is rejoicing with me, the wife of his youth. (Proverbs 5:18, my version)

> Love never fails. (1 Corinthians 13:8)

Often I would pray this prayer from Colossians 1:9–11, using our names:

> [I] continually ask God to fill [Philip and me] with the knowledge of his will through all the wisdom and understanding that the Spirit gives, so that [Philip and I] may live a life worthy of the Lord and please him in every way: bearing fruit in every good work, growing in the knowledge of God, being strengthened with all power according to his glorious might so that [Philip and I] may have great endurance and patience.

Again, I am not trying to make this sound like a platitude or to oversimplify real issues. I am just encouraging you to use the weapon that God has given you—His Word—to help you focus your thoughts on the truth, rather than letting worry weigh you down.[7]

There have been times in our marriage when I had to fight to get my thoughts under control, so this is not something we do once and then move on. This is a lifelong process—and a decision we must make each day. During another particularly difficult marriage season, I had a hard time even remembering the truth, much less declaring it. So I got on the phone with a friend I love and trust. She reminded me about what God says about marriage and men. She was frapping my life with ropes of hope and encouragement. And this leads us to the next brace: friends.

BRACE 2: EMBRACE THE PEOPLE GOD HAS PLACED IN YOUR LIFE

A few years ago my friend Kathy went through a severe financial storm. For years she had been a successful television producer, but suddenly the work dried up, and she encountered some unexpected expenses. She began to have more month than money. You may be able to relate! The facts did not look good. So she began to declare the truth. Because she is a tither, she knew that God would open windows of heaven and pour out a blessing so big that she wouldn't be able to contain it.[8] He would supply all that she needed according to His riches.[9]

Of course, she didn't just stay home and quote Scripture. She went out looking for work and continued to give of what she had.

However, Kathy had to learn to do something else in this particular storm. She had always been proud of the fact that, as a single mother, she had raised three smart and healthy kids without leaning on anyone else financially. It was wonderful that she had been so successful on her own, but in this storm, she needed to learn to ask for help. We are not designed to do life alone. King Solomon told us that two are better than one, because if one falls, the other will help.[10] The apostle Paul compared us to a human body, each part dependent on the other part. No one part can function alone, and no part is more important than the other.[11] We need all the parts. We need each other. The minute we think we can navigate a storm by ourselves, we are in trouble.

For Kathy, this was hard. She had to let go of her pride and humble herself. When she realized that she was going to lose her apartment, she finally reached out. Her friend was glad to share with her. Kathy got the help she needed and learned the value of relationships. She braced herself by embracing the people God had placed in her life.

We are part of an awesome company of women around the planet. You are not alone. Let me say that again: you are *not* alone. The heart-breaking reality is that so many people live isolated lives. While there are certainly no perfect people, there are those around you, in your school, your community, your church, who will bring strength to you and who will help you find your brave. You will fulfill what God created you to do only by getting and staying connected with those who join you on the journey. You were not created to solve all of life's problems on your own. You do not have all of the answers!

Together is a big deal to God. We were not created to function at our best in isolation. We were designed to function as a part of something bigger. We find our brave in being part of a team. A family. A community where everybody knows our name (and if you ever saw the TV sitcom *Cheers,* you are singing that line right now).

We have to get good at this. It is definitely not easy. Why? Because people are weird. People can be hard to get along with. People can hurt us. They don't do things our way. They don't see things our way. And yet God asks us to love one another. To work together as a body, to support each other, to be one another's brace. Just as the finger needs the hand and the leg needs a knee, we need one another. We won't get through the battles and challenges of life alone. We just won't. I know this because I tried.

I was raised to be independent. Just like toddlers, I wanted to do things "by myself." After the cancer diagnosis, I was going to be the strong one. I didn't want my family or friends to worry, so I did not show my fear. I let people know that I could handle the trips to get treatments on my own; I didn't need anyone to go with me. But too soon, I started to crumble. I really thought I could handle this by myself. I was wrong. Yes, I prayed. Yes, I spoke the truth of God's Word. But I needed something else. I needed the brace of other people in order to find my brave. One day while I was lying on my bed, I started to cry. Philip walked by and saw me. He crawled onto the bed and just held me. He said that he had wondered how long it was going to be before I broke. I finally asked him for help, which he wanted to give. Then he called friends, and from that moment on, I had company along the journey.

Sometimes in the animal kingdom, if one animal is suffering, it will go off by itself. However, a proverb tells us that she who isolates herself "rages against all wise judgment."[12] We can't go off by ourselves to lick our wounds. No! We have to give and get support from one another. Thank God for friends to help us get through. They provide a smile when ours is lost. They offer wisdom when we can't decide what to do. They bring chocolate because of course that helps everything. They drive us to doctor visits. They baby-sit our kids. They remind us that we are not forgotten and that we are very loved by God.

A few years ago, I went skiing with my children and a friend of my son's. Philip would have gone, but just the week before, he'd suffered a herniated disk, so he was home flat on his back. Since we had already paid for the trip, off I went with the kids! One day I decided to ski with the boys. Mistake number one. They like black-diamond runs, and the truth is, I am a casual, make-it-down-the-mountain-looking-at-beautiful-scenery-all-the-way-as-I-head-to-the-lodge-to-get-hot-chocolate kind of skier.

We got off the lift and quickly skied over a ledge. Mistake number two. I didn't look beyond the ledge before I actually went over it. When I landed on the other side, I quickly realized that I was in serious trouble. This run hadn't gotten a lot of snow, so bushes and trees were peeking through, not to mention the fact that it was an almost-vertical drop. My son and his friend were about a quarter of the way down by the time I caught my breath enough to scream. I was sure it was going to be my last day on earth, and I hadn't even given Philip a really good kiss before I left on the trip.

Jordan stopped and looked back at his crazy mother. Attempting not to cry, I knew there was *no way* I was going to make it down the hill. He and his friend climbed back up to me (I have no idea how), and we tried to figure out a way to get me to the bottom. Taking off my skis and sliding on my rear end was not an option; the slope was too steep and I would just roll, becoming the largest snowball in history as I crashed into bushes and trees. That did not sound fun. Eventually we came up with a plan—well, actually the boys did, while I mentally wrote my obituary.

We took off my skis, and I held on to a branch, putting my boots on Jordan's shoulders as a brace. Jordan uses blades, which are short, thicker skis—and that meant he could maneuver around bushes more easily. His friend held my skis, while my son had to bear my weight as well as the sharp points of my boots, as the three of us worked our way down the mountain. It was a slow process: me grabbing onto one branch at a time, my rear end in the snow, all the way down the mountain, with Jordan below me, keeping my feet on his shoulders. But they did it! Those boys got me safely down the hill. I was so grateful, I did a lot of hugging. They endured that, then Jordan calmly patted my shoulder and said, "We'll see you back at the room, Mom." Then they took off, as if they hadn't just saved my life. I don't remember the ski instructor mentioning the importance of the buddy system as he was teaching me to snowplow, but I am glad I had some buddies! Together *is* better.

What mountain are you trying to climb or get down from all by yourself? What stormy sea are you trying to navigate alone? Are you struggling to get free from an addiction but ashamed to reach out? Are you failing a class but embarrassed to ask for help?

While taking scuba-diving certification classes, I learned all about diving with a partner, not only because it is more fun, but it is also safer.

If something were to happen to my air tank, I could reach over and grab the extra regulator on my partner's vest and keep breathing. It's time for you to reach over and grab the regulator from a friend. Don't let potential embarrassment cause you to try to do this alone. You will find your brave in the company of others who are also finding their brave.

At times, as we go through storms, we will feel overloaded and overwhelmed, unable to remember what the truth is anymore. That's when we find our brave by doing what Paul and the crew did on their ship: brace ourselves. If we are going to make it to shore, we must use the support mechanisms God has provided. We can frap the hulls of our life by speaking the truth of God's Word and by seeking strength and help from our relationships.

3

Let It Go

A happy heart is good medicine and
a cheerful mind works healing.

—Proverbs 17:22, AMPC

Shake it off, I shake it off.

—Taylor Swift

I travel regularly. I have packed suitcases numerous times, but I still take too much. I don't notice it when someone else is carrying my bag, but if I have to haul it down the stairs to my car or up the stairs to the hotel room, I definitely feel the weight. My goal, as I pack, is always to take just enough. But I fail regularly. This is because, as I am packing, I think, *I might need this . . . and this . . . and that.* You never know! Most of the time I don't need whatever it was, so it just becomes extra weight in my bag.

Of course, I can't travel without my laptop and iPad, which means I have to bring all the necessary plugs, attachments, and accessories. I am sure I look burdened as I make my way through the airport. (I have friends who can travel for two weeks with only a carry-on . . . I try not to hate them.)

Most airlines limit each passenger's carry-on baggage to one bag and a purse (or briefcase). If you want to take more, you get charged. I know about their fees because I pay them. Regularly. I have often threatened myself that I will pitch my excess stuff!

Just as when we travel, in life we journey with far too much luggage. Perhaps, like me, you have gotten used to the baggage you carry; it has become a comfortable appendage. If you're going to make it through this storm, though, you must throw some of it overboard before the weight of it sinks you.

Throw It Overboard

The crew of the ship the apostle Paul was on had to deal with this same issue. The ship carried both passengers and cargo, since it had stopped at different ports of call and collected varied goods. During the storm, conditions on board went from bad to worse as the ship rocked and heaved, and the wind screamed and tore at everyone on deck. Seasickness and terrified grunts and yelps competed with the noise of the outside storm. And when nightfall descended, the blackness all around them, accompanied by the creaks and yowls, only brought additional terror. To make things worse, the cargo might have gotten loose and begun to slam against the sides of the ship. The crew must have realized that the boat could be torn apart not only by the waves but also by the cargo itself! They could be destroyed from the outside *and* the inside. In order to save the ship, they made a decision.

The sailors on Paul's ship had a smart idea for steadying their vessel: toss the excess overboard. Anything that wasn't essential for their survival got jettisoned.

What does this mean for us? It means that if we are to make it safely through our storms, then we need to toss out the excess baggage that weighs us down and makes the storm damage even worse. Believe it or not, there are things we cling to that are actually detrimental to us! We don't usually notice until a storm hits and we have to deal with the attitudes, the emotions, the pain, and the history that simply won't fit into a single carry-on. It's time to pitch the baggage overboard.

What do you need to dump? Maybe you need to see it in terms of life and death, just as the sailors on Paul's ship did. As Bible scholar Matthew Henry said, "Any man will rather make shipwreck of his goods than of his life."[1]

> They began to throw
> the cargo overboard.
> —Acts 27:18

Have you ever tried to endure a storm, only to realize that a hurricane is sweeping up from the south toward you? I have news for you: one is the storm; the other is actually the baggage you brought along with you. I'm talking about those past hurts, disappointments, fears, and insecurities that do nothing but bring you down.

In a lifetime of dealing with issues in my own soul, and more than thirty years ministering in a local church, I have learned to recognize some common baggage that we carry with us. Some are hidden in expensive Louis Vuitton or Tumi bags, but they are still baggage. They're heavy enough during the good weather of our lives, but they can be the difference between life and death during our storms.

Paul and the ship's crew were clear about what we need to do. Or if you are a lover of Disney's *Frozen,* feel free to sing it along with me: "Let it go!" (In my head I sound like Idina Menzel, the original vocalist. In reality, my voice lands somewhere between sounding like a frog and a dying cat.) Anyway, let's take a look at some of the baggage we need to jettison.

Past Hurts

Past hurts are pains you struggle with today, even though they originated in previous situations. The hurt might be rooted in a former marriage, a childhood disappointment, or a tragedy in your teens. You just haven't been able to deal with it or fix it yet. Or you've ignored it, hoping it will disappear on its own. Or perhaps you have dealt with it, but then something happened to trigger all of that old pain.

Sometimes in the face of crisis, you have had to shift into survival mode. Surviving is good. Surviving is better than being destroyed, but you don't want to keep living in survival mode. Perhaps you have started to distance yourself from others. In an attempt to be discerning, maybe you've actually become untrusting and overprotective. In trying to allow yourself time and space to heal, you've actually become unloving and unavailable. What once helped you to survive is now the baggage that is weighing you down—and can actually sink your boat.

I know someone who faced a storm in her dating life. After getting help, she realized that she was carrying issues from a disastrous past relationship. A man's actions had hurt her. He had vacillated between being hot and cold toward her. One moment he had said all the loving, beautiful words she wanted to hear, and the next moment he had been extremely unkind and borderline verbally abusive. Wisely she got out of that relationship. At first, she didn't want to date again—she wasn't sure she could trust a man again. Her survival mechanism was just to not go out. Then she realized she was developing an unhealthy attitude toward men. Eventually she did date again, but she found herself expecting the same bad behavior from her new guy, as if she were waiting for him to fail her. Her excess cargo was threatening to sink the relationship.

Past hurts often trigger behaviors that can destroy our todays. Consider my husband's family of origin. His parents had a volatile marriage, which ultimately ended in divorce. Their arguments were so loud and violent that police were often called to the house. This obviously affected

Philip: he hated confrontation because, in his experience, any conflict was a threat and would eventually blow up. So he backed away from any disagreement, which led to serious issues within our marriage.

Some of my past hurts came from my school years. I grew up thinking that perfect grades and perfect behavior were required to be accepted and loved. Honestly, I am not sure why. I don't remember my parents harping on my grades; I just internally put this pressure on myself. Maybe I liked the affirmation good grades and good behavior brought, and so I came to the conclusion that my performance was essential to my being loved. The burden I put on myself in school almost became too much to bear. This became baggage that I needed to throw overboard (more about this in the next chapter).

Past hurts can take up excessive amounts of space in our hearts. It's as if we carry Russian Matryoshka dolls within us. Somewhere in my travels I picked up some of these wooden nesting dolls. Inside the big one is a smaller one. And inside that one is another even smaller one. Each one contains a tinier doll until you get down to the most minuscule carved doll. You can stand them in a line, side by side, and each one is just slightly smaller than the previous one.

Painful experiences are like that set of dolls; each hurt comes with its own set of luggage, and each stuffs itself into the next. Most of us have been betrayed at some point. If we haven't dealt with it, we carry the baggage of bitterness. If we don't deal with that bitterness, it breeds unforgiveness. And the unforgiveness breeds resentment. And the resentment creates envy. And envy harbors distrust. Look at all those Russian dolls! All that baggage! If we don't lighten our load and intentionally lose some of this stuff, we can spend the rest of our lives crippled by the weight.

I am an extrovert, so I find it easy to open my heart and life to people. With that also comes the risk of hurt, and I have been wounded a few times.

- People said one thing and did another.
- People were careless with my feelings and my heart.

- People said unkind things about me.
- People allowed misunderstandings to drive a wedge between us.
- People remained silent when I had hoped they would have my back.

Each one felt like a punch to the gut. In an upcoming chapter I will share how difficult the past year of my life has been. So many hurtful situations. I would get through one, take a deep breath, then stick my head and heart out again, only to be hit from another direction. After a few of these, I wanted to stay in my room and cry. Really. Me, the extrovert, did not want to be with people. I allowed cynicism to take root in my soul. Cynicism became unforgiveness that became bitterness. My own little set of nesting dolls. Only they weren't the cute Russian ones I could display on my dresser. They were the ugly, nasty, heavy ones. And they needed to go.

So how do we get rid of the power past hurts hold over us? By practicing forgiveness. Whatever its source, in order to get rid of the baggage of past pain, we have to be willing to forgive—sincerely and deeply—those who have hurt us.

Honestly, most of the time, I have to work at it. I think I'm doing pretty well by just not killing someone. But I get the feeling Jesus wants us to be overachievers in this area of forgiveness.

The bottom line: forgiveness takes practice and determination. It requires us to find our brave. To excel in it, to actually let go of the pain, requires an act of will. I never feel like forgiving. In fact, I feel like smacking the person who hurt me!

When I endure the sting of betrayal, I feel justified in my hurt. But I don't want this piece of baggage to sink my ship, so I decide to forgive. Daily. Until the pain goes away. I say it out loud, "I forgive _____ for _____." When that person comes to mind and if the thought of that person still brings pain, I say it again. I keep doing that until it doesn't hurt. I ask God to help me forgive and let it go. This could take days, weeks, or months. And I remind myself that I have been forgiven much, so really, who am I to hold on to any offense? Jesus told us to forgive our enemies,[2] so I am sure I don't have the right to stay bitter and unforgiving toward anyone.

Choosing forgiveness is like putting medicine on our wounds. The process stings (a lot) sometimes, but it brings thorough healing. Find your brave. Throw that bag of past hurts overboard!

DISAPPOINTMENTS AND UNMET EXPECTATIONS

The ache of disappointment, in itself, can be as devastating as any violent act. When you have set your heart on something, not achieving it can become a poison that contaminates the very blood that flows through your heart. Most of us harbor unrealistic expectations. As William Shakespeare put it, "Expectation is the root of all heartache."

Disappointment comes in many forms, from the not-so-big-of-a-deal to the devastating:

The Chicago Cubs fan who longs for a championship.

The high school athlete who didn't make the team.

The college graduate who can't find the right job.

The childless woman who has turned forty and still yearns for a baby.

The man who always wanted to start his own business and who sees that his window of opportunity is no longer open.

The teenage girl who has not realized her own beauty, staring at the Photoshopped images in the magazine and realizing that she will never look like them.

The woman who suffers through yet another bad first date in a series of really bad first dates.

The young man with his eyes on a certain career who fails interview after interview.

The mom with three kids who struggles to take a shower and get everybody dressed by day's end and wonders where the day went.

Life is hard, isn't it? And it becomes even harder when we don't know how to let go of unfulfilled expectations.

I've discovered a few steps to getting rid of the baggage of disappointment.

First, you can't take everything personally. While you have to take personal responsibility for some of your disappointments—because maybe you didn't invest the time in studying for the GRE, for instance, so you didn't get into grad school, or you stayed out too late playing, overslept, and missed the job interview—you also have to recognize that not everything is your fault. Sometimes the reality is, life will simply do what it does.

When you take something personally, it needlessly narrows your point of view and prevents you from gaining wisdom, which is an ability to see life from a richer more meaningful perspective. Which leads us to the next step.

Second, review your expectations. When you take a good look at your expectations, you will get closer to a truer understanding of the event. Perhaps your expectations were unrealistic. Perhaps they could be adjusted to cope with this new reality. Either way, now is the time to question whether these expectations actually serve you or sink you.[3]

Third, see the big picture by putting your hope in God and the promise that He has all things under control. Friends will let you down; only God will never fail you or forsake you.[4] The goal is maturity, and maturity does not necessarily come from how much we know or how old we are, but rather from how we navigate trials. As James wrote, "Consider it pure joy, my brothers and sisters, whenever you face trials of many kinds, because you know that the testing of your faith produces perseverance. Let perseverance finish its work so that you may be mature and complete, not lacking anything."[5]

Both James and Paul assure us that problems and hardships produce strength of character.[6] As believers, we stand perfect before God, but our maturity is progressive. This may not seem like good news, especially if you are dealing with the pain of disappointment. Many times this last year as I was weighed down by one disappointment after another, I sang the words that Horatio Spafford wrote, "When sorrows [disappointments] like sea billows roll; Whatever my lot, Thou hast taught me to say: It is well, it is well with my soul."

Disappointment can be replaced only with hope. Put your hope in the God who will see you through this and "give you the desires of your heart."[7] We can have a hope that does not lead to disappointment even as we walk through the hard times, because we can know how much we are loved by God and that He *will* see us through.

FEAR

Fear is a powerful piece of baggage that can seriously hold us back. Fear is such a debilitating force. It has an amazing power to magnify problems, make everything appear worse than it really is, and force on us the negative and hopeless. And then, like a self-fulfilling prophecy, fear causes our distorted view of life to become our reality.

The symbol for the dramatic arts is two masks: one with a big smile, and one with tears. Faith and fear are like that. They are like twin brothers who live in the same house. Their voices are similar. They both look something like their parent—you. Sometimes it's difficult to tell one from the other. And they both wield power in your life. So where you put your energy and your focus is crucial.

In the year after my cancer diagnosis, I had to go back to the oncologist for a checkup. I felt fine. I wasn't worried as I got in the car and drove to the appointment. As soon as I got to his office and walked down the hall, fear filled my heart. I remembered the diagnosis the year before and the anxiety of that initial doctor visit came rushing back. My heart pounded, I couldn't catch my breath, and I was afraid of what I would hear.

There was no logical reason for my fear. I had no pain and no symptoms of cancer. And yet in that moment I had to find my brave and throw fear overboard. I took a breath and reminded myself that "God has not given [me] a spirit of fear."[8] No matter what the outcome, He would never leave me.

I don't know how many years I have left on earth, but I am not going to live afraid of what a doctor will tell me.

At that appointment and in the ten years of appointments since then, I have gotten the all clear. Yay! How much of my precious life and energy would I have wasted giving in to fear?

But what if I *had* heard something different? What would be the worst-case scenario? Another cancer diagnosis? Death? I would have to find my brave and trust God through that battle too. And really our worst-case scenario only leads to our best eternity. Obviously, I want to live lots of years. I have plans for all of those years to come. I am just not going to live them afraid of what might happen. As my friend Bob Goff recently posted on his Instagram feed, "Anxiety never leaves a ransom note when it steals our lives; fear is a punk."

I had to find my brave again when it seemed as if each week this past year brought bad news to the point that I started to fear answering the phone. When someone said they needed to see me, I became afraid of what I would hear. Once again, with each new situation, I had to remind myself to ditch the fear.

Many people I encounter are controlled by fear. People make more decisions out of fear than any other emotion. A woman I know was so afraid of failure that she wouldn't even apply to college. Another young woman was so afraid of being alone that she married the first guy who paid any attention to her. He was not a good guy. But we have a choice. We can feed our fear or feed our faith. The one we feed is the one that will flourish. The energy and attention we give to one will diminish the other.

I'm not trying to make this simplistic, but we do decide where our thoughts go. I can let my fear cause me to dwell on pictures of me failing, or I can trust that God is with me on this journey and will not leave me.

The Enemy loves it when our fear immobilizes us and keeps us from finding our brave and taking steps toward freedom. Don't let him win!

I knew a couple who were working on their marriage. It was marriage number two for the wife, and the relationship was turbulent. When they came to Philip and me for help, we discovered that the problem in this current storm was actually based in her first marriage. It had been volatile, with lots of yelling and fighting, and then after all the screaming, he would just walk out the door. She came out of that marriage hurt and afraid.

When she married again, at first she buried those emotions and refused to argue or even express an opinion. Well, that lasted only a few months, and then, as in most marriages, the differences surfaced and the conflict started. Rather than deal with any of it, she withdrew. She thought if she just didn't say anything, this marriage would be okay. Living with her fears from her previous marriage, she believed this husband would disappear if they argued.

The thing is, this husband had no intention of disappearing. He wanted to work on their marriage, and he didn't understand why she wouldn't talk. When we brought the issue to light, she began to deal with her fear. She realized that it would sink her marriage if she held on to it.

You are painting the picture of your life. The energy you give to either faith or fear will color your world and create the emotional accents of the painting you are creating. Which color do you want to add to your masterpiece: faith or fear?

Letting go of the baggage of fear takes a determined desire to focus on the promises of God. We get to choose what we believe and what we focus on. In many of the psalms, King David wrote we should magnify the Lord. The meaning of *magnify* is simple: "make God big." Make His promises larger than life. Focus on His promises until they are larger than the problem we face. His promises are inspiring. They encourage us when we apply them to our individual circumstances. When those promises become our personal sources of hope, they can drastically transform our attitudes. (For a list of some of God's awesome promises that you can focus on, look at "Scriptures to Speak over Your Situation" at the back of this book.)

David faced Goliath with faith in his heart, a song in his mouth, and a far-greater-than-his-fear picture of God. In this story we read that David ran "quickly" to meet Goliath.[9] He could run quickly because he wasn't going in his strength or on the merit of his name, but in the name of his God and in His might.

After Joshua and Caleb encountered giants in the Promised Land, they went back and told the others that they needed to go "at once" to claim their inheritance.[10]

It is not good to look at what you fear for too long. Staring at the pool from the top of the diving platform won't get rid of the fear of diving in. Staring at the outside of your coworker's door won't make the tough conversation ahead of you any easier.

You and I will be faced with fear.

Fear of failure. Fear of defeat. Fear of the future. Fear of the unknown. Fear of the "what ifs." Fear of people. Fear of death.

And if we give in to it, we will discover what fear really does. Fear debilitates. It stops us in our tracks. It keeps us from fulfilling our purpose. It is the ultimate weapon of the Enemy to keep us from our mission. In all its forms, fear must be conquered.

Every hero of the Bible encountered fear. And every one of them who praised God destroyed the fear when they lifted their hands and voices to the great I Am.

And every modern-day hero (hello, that's you) encounters fear. And we destroy it when we lift our voices to the King of kings. When we praise our God, we acknowledge His awesomeness, His majesty, His kingdom, and His cause. We proclaim that He is God and we are not. There's a thought.

Find your brave. Pitch the baggage of fear overboard by turning your focus to God.

THE "THREE-I'D" BAGGAGE MONSTER

Perhaps the subtlest piece of baggage we carry is actually a three-in-one monster: Insufficiency, Insignificance, and Insecurity.

You are an important instrument in the plan of God. He has created you out of the inspiration of His love. He has designed you to enjoy a life of fulfillment and significance. Yet somehow you may have allowed your experiences, others' comments, and your feelings to shape your view of yourself, which has left you with very little confidence in who you actually are.

The writer of Hebrews told us not to "throw away" our confidence because "it will be richly rewarded."[11] God created us with amazing ability and potential, yet so many of us are riddled with questions like the following:

Am I important?

Do I have what it takes to make a difference?

Do others value me and my contributions?

Can I be accepted and respected if I am myself?

Do I matter?

When, at the core of our souls, these questions assail us, our insecurities have no answer to offer. At best, we may meekly whisper, "I hope so."

As we process these questions, a "three-I'd" monster lurks within this piece of baggage. His name is Insufficiency, Insignificance, and Insecurity. He is the Goliath in our lives. He stands tall, mocking, and threatening. His victims are obvious and numerous.

Insufficiency shouts, "You don't have enough education, money, or talent. You don't have enough faith. Someone else could accomplish something, but not you. You have *almost* enough skill. If you had just a bit more experience or time or friends or talent or . . . Nope, let's be honest here; you just aren't up to the challenge."

Insignificance chimes in, "If you were taller, more gifted, or more educated—maybe. But you aren't. And no one really needs you. You are not that important to the team. You are not right for the part. You aren't enough."

. Insecurity is the result. He whispers, "Well, you did fail that other time. It probably is true—you can't do this either. Your God cannot help you. You are going to lose, and you should just accept it. Be careful that you don't think you are more important than you are. It is time to surrender to what you secretly suspected all along."

Ditch this baggage!

Repeat this after me: "God said that I am wonderfully made. I am His masterpiece. I have value. In fact, He says my value is 'far above rubies or pearls.'"[12]

You and I are His daughters, which makes us princesses. It is crucial that we understand that we are the glorious, delightful, irreplaceable, irresistible, loved-beyond-measure daughters of the King. As His masterpieces, we are created by Him with specific strengths and abilities to do His work on the earth. When we don't understand this, we carry around the baggage of insecurity, and this cargo will sink us in any storm.

We all have insecurities that need to be thrown overboard. Insecurity distorts your judgment, brings confusion, and negatively affects your relationships with others.

Sometimes, rather than admitting or dealing with our own insecurities, we attack others who are confident. Their confidence exposes our "three-I'd" monster. We *all* struggle with jealousy. Our world grooms us to compare ourselves to one another. From reality shows to beauty pageants, from politics to business, rarely are we pooling our gifts and working together. Usually we work hard to win. We silently compete to be the first or the best or the one who is right. But this is not the way of the kingdom of God. In the way of Christ, there is room for all of us to be who He has called us to be.[13]

I knew two women—we'll call them Jenny and Gaby—whose friendship was growing . . . and then they encountered a storm. While she wouldn't admit it at first, Gaby was jealous of Jenny. Most things seemed to come easy to Jenny: achieving academic honors, finding a husband, having children, and building a successful career. The truth is, Jenny worked as hard as anyone to gain what she enjoyed in life. But to Gaby, it just didn't seem fair. She couldn't even find a nice guy to date. Her biological clock was ticking. She felt unsatisfied at work, never believing she was doing a good job. The proverbial straw came when Jenny received a promotion. Gaby tried to be happy about it, but Jenny could tell that it wasn't genuine, and so she began to pull away from the friendship.

When I talked to Gaby, we realized that Jenny wasn't the first friend with whom she'd had problems. Her feelings of inadequacy, insignificance, and insecurity had produced jealousy again and again, and she lost more than one friend because of it. This is a common situation because everything in our culture pits us against one another. Social media does not help. We compare the amount and kind of followers we have. We monitor the "likes" on our Facebook posts and pictures. We compare the kind of life we live with the one our friend portrays in her Instagram feed.

When we lack confidence, when we wrestle with insecurity, we will be unstable and anxious in many areas of our lives. Our feelings of insecurity will destroy relationships. To erase such feelings, we have to find our brave and see ourselves as the masterpiece of our Creator. Yes, it takes work. I understand the battle it is. But throwing that bag of insecurity overboard is a battle worth fighting. If the enemy of our soul, Satan, can keep us doubting who we really are, then we will remain burdened by weights that will sink us.

In order for another friend of mine, Jan, to ditch her insecurity, she had to tell herself the truth. "I finally had to bring it all the way down to the fact that I believed a lie," she told me. "My lie was that I must take care of myself. If anything good was going to happen, or if anything bad was going to be prevented, somehow it was up to me. In the smallest places in me, I was still an afraid little girl, trying to control every nuance of a situation in order to produce a result that would receive the approval of a father."

What are the lies you believe?

Insecurity can be a heavy bag to throw overboard. You *can* change the picture you have of yourself. You can "be transformed by the renewing of your mind."[14] Have hope; it is possible. If you are going to find your brave and weather your storm, you must.

The Bible tells us to give all our worries and cares to God, and that we can pile our troubles on God's shoulders. He'll carry our loads. He'll help us.[15] What a picture. God invites us to put our load on Him. It's an exchange program. We trade our load for His, and His load "is light."[16] Good deal!

It takes bravery to drop the bags you've gotten comfortable carrying around. And you will find a whole new level of brave as you walk free of them. You will have a fresh sense of strength to navigate this storm. So c'mon, drop the baggage—all of it—before it sinks you.

Keep the Main Thing the Main Thing

Good things happen when you set your priorities straight.

—Scott Caan

I always told God, "I'm going to hold steady on You, an' You've got to see me through."

—Harriet Tubman

Sometimes reevaluating our meaning and value can be extremely clarifying and freeing. It sounds intense and might give you a headache, but asking yourself the right questions can be a life-altering exercise. The old question "If your house caught on fire and you could save only three things, what would they be?" is supposed to help us see what really matters to us.

A few years ago, when the fires raged in Southern California, I asked myself that question. Those fires destroyed almost four thousand homes and eight hundred thousand acres, and one was burning out of control about a mile from my house.

I had to ask myself, *If we have to evacuate, what should I take?*

Photos? You know, the ones in an actual album—before iPhoto was around.

Clothes?

Important papers? *Where are those?*

As I wrestled with those questions and began stuffing photos and a file cabinet in my car, the fire changed direction. Someone in another neighborhood now had to ask those same questions.

In the last chapter we talked about throwing overboard all the emotional baggage that threatens to sink us. Some other things that are actually good to have during easy times can become burdensome during the storms. So it's important to figure out what else needs to go and what we need to keep. So let's talk about priorities, which will keep us on track as we head toward our shore.

Lightening More of the Load

In the previous chapter we saw that, in order to lighten their load initially, the sailors on Paul's ship tossed the cargo overboard. But that wasn't enough. They needed to continue to lighten the load if they were going to make it through the storm.

> They threw the ship's tackle
> overboard with their own hands.
>
> —Acts 27:19

They now had to throw the ship's equipment over the side to further ease the weight of the vessel and keep it from hitting a sand bar. They ejected the main sail and the extra gear. All of that would have been nice to have on the journey, but when the situation became life or death, the sailors got rid of it. Their main priority was doing what was necessary to brave their way through the storm in order to reach the shore alive.

Too often in the middle of our storms, we use up our best energy on insignificant activities, like worrying or trying to make everyone happy or trying to figure it all out or worrying (did I say that already?), or even on the trivial—such as obsessing over how many followers we have on social media or shopping for another pair of shoes (my bad).

Some of the things we hold on to aren't bad, such as the desire for a new car or the trip to Europe, but when they threaten your ship in a storm, it may be time to rethink those priorities. We need to follow Stephen Covey's advice: "The main thing is to keep the main thing, the main thing."[1]

Easier said than done, I know. When we are in a storm, we have only so much energy. If we want to survive the storm, part of finding our brave is discerning the main thing and keeping it . . . yep, the main thing—and then not focusing on the rest. Because it doesn't really matter.

At a staff meeting a few years ago, my husband asked for volunteers to help illustrate a point. After gathering the three innocent victims at the front of the room, he gave them their roles: "You are all firefighters. Your job is to put out fires." Then he explained that since there were no fires that day, he was going to give each one a responsibility. "Volunteer One, wash the truck. Number Two, mop the floor. And Number Three, wrap up the hoses neatly."

He had them mime their particular jobs, poked fun at them, and then demanded that they act out their imaginary tasks more convincingly. It was entertaining, and we had a lot of laughs. Then he asked each of them, "What was your job again?" They responded in turn, "Wash the truck." "Mop the floor." "Wrap up the hoses."

Then he drove home his point. "No. You are all wrong. Your job is to put out fires." He had deliberately put so much focus on the other tasks so that we all had forgotten what their real job and priority was: to put out fires.

In life, we can lose our way when we allow things, whether good and interesting or bad and destructive, to slowly and subtly become priorities. In a storm, remembering and focusing on our priorities is a matter of survival. Just as the main sail on Paul's ship didn't serve the crew during the storm and they needed to chuck it, so we need to live every day asking ourselves, *What's the most important thing?* I know this seems obvious, but in my years of ministry I have seen people do the wildest things simply because, in the midst of a storm, they forgot what their priorities were.

STOP PURSUING THE TRIVIAL THINGS

Trivial Pursuit has been a popular game over the years. It is based on our knowledge of facts that have little impact on our quality of life. It's a fun game, but living our lives in pursuit of the trivial is not!

To many people, trivial pursuit is not a game; it's a lifestyle. Sometimes we are more concerned about a celebrity news story or our friend's social media stream than we are about our own ups and downs. Someone else's drama can be so involving, so alluring, that we forget to focus on the priorities in our own lives.

Storms can be disorienting. In the confusion and chaos of a dark, scary moment, we can be tempted to do things that numb our pain. We play hours of Candy Crush Saga or avoid dealing with our own agony by watching the Kardashians. I am not saying that you can't have a moment or two or ten to unwind and decompress. Just for how long?

In the midst of the heartache of this last year, I chose to end many of my hard days by watching movies where stuff blew up (I'm not sure what that says about me . . .) or reading spy novels that involved lots of bad guys being caught. In the midst of a storm, it is normal to look for what feels good momentarily. I couldn't control the waves, so I wanted to control the moment. Candy Crush and spy novels are not horrible things. But some choices are. Getting drunk, smoking weed, or sleeping with some guy might numb the ache momentarily, but the consequences will create another storm. So let's find our brave, and let's work hard to remember our priorities, even as wave after wave crashes against us. I can't tell you what all of your personal priorities should be, but I can offer biblical priorities we all should hang on to as we face our challenges.

PRIORITY 1: HONOR GOD

Jesus gave us simple but profound direction about keeping the main thing the main thing. He told us to seek first the kingdom of God.[2] We need to do what God wants us to do. In a storm or on calm seas, we should always do what honors God. This priority helps us sort through all the options that bombard our thinking when a coworker lies about us, when our child is accused of bullying, or when our car gets rear-ended. We might want to lash out as the waves hit, but if we keep honoring God as our first priority, then we won't allow our emotions and others' desires to distract us. We don't want to lose sight of what we're really here to do.

As I have mentioned, Philip and I struggled through some rough periods, and many times what kept me headed in the right direction was doing my best to honor God. In some moments those lovin' feelings weren't there; it seemed like coldness and anger had settled in my heart. I knew that I could let those feelings propel me down a path that would only lead to destruction or I could choose to make decisions that honored God, like communicating with respect when I felt like rolling my eyes or shutting my mouth when I wanted to defend my opinion. I could demonstrate love when I wasn't feelin' it, or I could walk away. Time and again, I chose to love and seek unity. And he did too. Shockingly, I am not always easy to love. The rewards weren't immediate, but they did come—all because we decided what we needed to keep in our marriage boat (God-honoring responses) and what we needed to pitch overboard (gut-level reactions).

Part of honoring God is making difficult decisions in which we find ourselves at odds with what we thought were our priorities. I moved to

Los Angeles in the 1980s to work as an actress. I was thrilled to land a job on a nighttime soap opera. Remember this was the '80s, when big hair and soap operas ruled. In this show I was the "young thing," which basically meant I was in lingerie or a bikini for most of the scenes. The show was fairly popular; the way it was produced was unique and so it garnered a lot of media attention. I had not been in Los Angeles long and had only begun to get serious about my relationship with God. After the show was finished filming, I felt God tell me that He hadn't given me a gift for me to use it in a show that highlighted immorality.

In that moment, I decided to be discriminating about the parts I would take. There weren't many roles that actually honored God, but I knew I could at least start with the roles that didn't dishonor Him. Of course that commitment was tested soon after I made it. I auditioned for a part in a TV show and was given a scene to read with the casting director. I could tell that she liked my reading. On my way out I asked for the whole script, so I could find out just what kind of show this was.

I went home, read the script, and discovered it was another nighttime soap opera, filled with what is typical in that genre. Because of the commitment I had made to God, I knew that I couldn't do the show. I basically forgot about it and went on with my life—until I got a call from my manager that the show's producers wanted me to come back that afternoon. I let her know that I would not go to the callback because it was not a show I wanted to do. She did not understand and was frustrated as we hung up.

Later that week, she called me, excited because they wanted to screen test me for the show. They had auditioned hundreds of girls for the part and wanted to screen test three of them. I was one of the three. I had to let her know that while I was honored, I would not do that show. She hung up on me.

The next week she called me elated. "Holly, you are so smart. Way to go holding out on them! They are now offering you the part. They don't need to see you again; they are just giving it to you." She named a salary that made my head spin. I was so surprised! This does not happen. To get a part, an actor has to go on several auditions as the producers and director narrow the group. To go from one initial audition to being offered the part was highly unusual.

This was that rubber-meets-the-road time. Was I serious about my decision to honor God? Even some of my Christian friends encouraged me to take the part! They told me, "Everybody has to start somewhere, and if you want to ever have influence in this town, you have to take parts like this."

I just couldn't do it. I knew what God had asked me to do. So once again I told my manager that I would pass. My manager, who only made money when I did, was angry.

A few days later, my manager called me laughing. She said, "You are not going to believe this, but they have doubled their salary offer to you! They really want you, and this will definitely help set up your future."

She stopped laughing when I let her know that it did not matter how much they were going to pay me; I was not going to do this show. I had to face my brave in those moments because, by saying no, I was potentially entering a major financial storm. But I knew that God had to be my main priority—even above my career.

That was more than thirty years ago, and I have never regretted that decision. I made a living as an actress for a few more years, playing roles that honored my commitment to God. I did not know then that one day I would be a pastor in a church filled with actors; I was just honoring God in that moment. And He has used my experience to encourage others to honor God, to keep Him and His kingdom as their priorities.

What decision is before you today? In what ways can you keep His kingdom a priority? Telling the truth when that "white" lie would be so much easier? Apologizing for swearing at your coworker? Choosing joy when you don't know how this situation will turn out? Saying no to a job that would take you away from your family for months? Honoring God means putting His will first. Find your brave and choose to do that.

But it doesn't stop there and the apostle Paul understood this. As he mentored Timothy, his son in the faith, he told him to remember that "the goal of our instruction is love [which springs] from a pure heart and a good conscience and a sincere faith."[3] Every one of our goals or investments should build one of these three priority areas: love from a pure heart, a good conscience, and sincere faith.

PRIORITY 2: LOVE FROM A PURE HEART

A Pharisee asked Jesus, "Of all the commandments, which is the most important?"

Jesus replied, "'Love the Lord your God with all your heart and with all your soul and with all your mind and with all your strength.' The second is this: 'Love your neighbor as yourself.'"[4]

That's what priorities are all about: loving God and loving people. Let's keep it simple. First, even in the middle of a storm, don't lose your love for God. It's a priority. We can't live a joyful and fulfilling life without God. Hold on to your love for Him. Pursue His love. So many make the mistake of throwing out the most important aspect of life: a relationship with God. His love is not expendable.

I know there are people who get angry with God and walk away from Him during a crisis. They blame Him for their struggles and pain. But finding our brave means standing firm in our faith. I had a friend whose child had cancer, and she told me, "Where else could I turn? I am in pain, and I would rather be in pain turning to God than away from Him."

I know you might have questions about why this storm is happening. I do too. Maybe even doubts. I do too. I hope the questions and doubts drive you to the love of God, rather than away.

Second, in the midst of your trial, keep running toward relationships, toward loving the people in your world. I know it is easy to get frustrated with them when they don't understand what you're going through. When work or school or a friendship is tough, remember that the people in your world are the priority. Just go home and love on your family, or go out with your girlfriends, or grab coffee with a coworker. People are always more important than things or situations.

The Beatles sang, "All You Need Is Love." And yep, this is the core of our faith. Are you in the midst of a storm, and you can't figure out what to do? Do what communicates love. Maybe it is giving a gift or saying a kind word. Or maybe it is simply listening to another person who is in the middle of her own storm. Why? Just because we're in a storm doesn't mean the world is supposed to revolve around us! Loving others often works to get us out of our self-centered pain and aware of how God wants to use us to help others.

A few years ago I boarded a small plane to head to a speaking engagement. The only flight attendant on the plane greeted me as I entered. She was young and as we chatted I found she was fairly new with the company. I laughingly told her that I was an old pro at flying and that if she needed help I was available. Soon after I took my seat, a woman with long, red, curly hair boarded. I was immediately aware of her because I love long, red, curly hair. Really. In heaven I just might have long, red, curly hair. My husband says that it won't happen, but I asked him how he knows. While I was distracted by the beautiful red hair, I heard this woman start verbally attacking the young flight attendant. She complained about the carry-on space in the small plane, complained about the delay, and basically complained about everything else. I could tell the flight attendant was having a hard time, and I was starting to get upset on her behalf. The woman angrily marched down the aisle to her seat. Guess where she stopped? You guessed it. At my aisle. Right next to me. Joy. After she got settled, I felt a whisper from heaven.

Holly, ask her how she is doing.

No, I silently whispered back. *You ask her how she is doing.*

Silence.

I knew what God wanted me to do.

I looked at her and finally said, "How are you today?"

"Fine." Her reply was curt.

See, God, she is fine.

Only, as I looked at her, she didn't look fine. So I asked her again. "How are you? Really?"

She took a deep breath and then told me that she had recently been told that she had a fatal disease, and now she was headed home to get things in order.

Wow.

We chatted for a while; I prayed for her and let her cry. And I apologized to God for my initial unwillingness to love on someone who seemed to be hard to love. Love from a pure heart sometimes involves bravely being stretched into uncomfortable areas of loving people. But this is a priority worth keeping.

PRIORITY 3: KEEP A GOOD CONSCIENCE

The storms we ride out are difficult enough without having to deal with guilt and shame as well. We have the incredible privilege of confessing our sins and weaknesses to the Father and being forgiven. Then even though we might be battered by waves, we can at least sail through the storm with a clean conscience.

I have made some bad decisions in my life. As a college student I put a lot of pressure on myself to make great grades. Only As and a few Bs were acceptable. The first semester of my freshman year, I made the dean's list and was well on my way to doing the same in the second semester. But then I received a C on a test in my biology class. Definitely not acceptable.

As I looked over the test, I saw a simple mistake that I had made on a diagram. If I hadn't messed that up, I would have gotten a B, so I just changed one of the lines on the diagram and submitted it for a re-grade. According to the professor's policy, a student could submit a test to be graded again if he or she felt a test had not been graded fairly. Only in this case, I submitted an altered version of my original test. I cheated. I left the class, walked back to my dorm, and within moments, the weight of what I had done crushed me. My conscience was screaming. I guess the good news is that I still had one. I tossed and turned in bed that night. If I had kept the main thing the main thing—to honor God and keep a clear conscience—I would not have cheated.

Unbeknownst to me, the professor's policy was also to randomly select a few students and make copies of their original tests, and then compare the original to the one submitted for the re-grade. Mine was one of the tests randomly chosen.

The next day the professor asked me to stay after class. I was busted! He had my original test and the one I had submitted to be graded again. I was in trouble. This university had a zero-tolerance policy with regard to cheating; I could have been kicked out, all because I had not made a priority of keeping a good conscience. Fortunately, a few other professors spoke up for me at a hearing, and I was able to stay at that school. I learned my lesson.

It took me a while to forgive myself, to let go of the shame. And I'm not alone in that. The Bible has stories of people who had to let go of shame in order to move forward.

One of the most amazing stories was one that Jesus told: the parable of the prodigal son.[5] The story is about a father and his two sons. The younger son wants to leave home and take his inheritance with him. The father agrees to his request, and so the boy takes off. In a short while the boy runs out of money, having spent it carelessly (possibly on parties and prostitutes). To survive, he ends up feeding pigs, and he is so hungry that the pig slop looks good. He finally realizes that even the servants on his father's farm are treated better than he is, so he decides to go home. But he doesn't feel worthy of being his father's son. He returns home, bent over with shame. The father responds by embracing him and throwing a party. He lets his son see he is glad the boy has returned. He not only accepts the boy, but he also lets him know that he is important—and still beloved. His forgiveness removes the shame.

The father is the picture of God, always with open arms ready to welcome us home. He forgives us, and then we have to let go of the shame and the guilt. Finding our brave sometimes means responding with humility when we have messed up, asking God for His forgiveness, and then resolving to make decisions that lead to a good conscience.

So many people feel that deep sense of unworthiness, guilt, or shame—whether because of their failures or some mistaken conclusion they have reached in their own minds. After the cheating incident, I had to continue to forgive myself, knowing that I was forgiven. I know you might be thinking, *Cheating? Really? That isn't such a big deal! I've done far worse than that.* And maybe you have. The thing is, sin is sin. And regardless of what it is, it produces shame and guilt. And the only antidote is to go to Jesus and seek forgiveness from Him. It is a priority that we live with a clear conscience, which means we need to make decisions that produce that, and when we fail, we get our clear conscience by running back into the arms of our heavenly Father, knowing that His forgiveness makes us clean again.

PRIORITY 4: PURSUE A SINCERE FAITH

Having sincere faith, a genuine trust in God, is another essential priority. It is a faith that affects how we live every single day. It is a faith that we can apply to our real-life situations.

I have seen smart people who have studied the Bible but nevertheless just don't seem to know God. When a real challenge in their career comes, they wilt, because while they have the knowledge, they don't have sincere faith that God will see them through. They keep looking for intellectual answers. It is not just knowledge that will get you through the storm but faith in Him.

We show our faith not only in what we believe but also by how we demonstrate that belief. We should be known as people of faith not only by what we say but also by the way we live. My faith shouldn't just be evidenced by how many Bible verses I've memorized but by how many verses I *live*.

One time while watching a music awards show, I saw a young man win for one of his songs. While he was certainly talented, his particular style was vulgar, crude, perverted, and degrading to women. None of that shocked me; I know all kinds of music are out there. What did shock me was his response after receiving the award. As he held up his treasure, he thanked his "Lord and Savior, Jesus Christ."

How sad. Maybe he should ask for Jesus's help the next time he writes a song! There is obviously no integrity between what he believes and how he lives. He is not excelling in faith. It made me look at my own actions. Is the faith I profess evident in what I do?

Honestly, there have been many times my faith could use some work. I find it easy to trust God on the good days, but sometimes when I come face to face with my humanity, especially in the midst of the toughest times, I fail the faith test. I had to work hard this last year to keep the main thing the main thing.

Without a genuine faith, not only is it "impossible to please God,"[6] but it will be very hard to endure when gale-force winds blow. Find your brave by making real faith a priority!

GETTING BACK TO THE BASICS

Both of my children have played basketball, and I have been to many practices and watched as their coaches worked to inspire them. Imagine this: A basketball coach meets with his team at halftime. They have just finished the worst half game of the entire season. They have made numerous mental errors, and they've failed to run plays they spent hours practicing. They are so bad that they look as if they don't even know how to play the game, and the score shows it.

The coach looks at his players, not even sure exactly where to start. Finally he says, "Okay, guys, let's start with the priorities. This orange ball is a basketball. Our first job is to put it into our basket. Second, we want to keep the other team from putting the ball into its basket. I'm not sure what you were trying to do out there, but let's just focus on these two priorities."

Can you imagine Jesus sitting down with us in our locker room and saying, "You're getting off track. This is the Bible. These words should guide you in loving God and loving each other."

As you face your storm, rather than freak out, remember the important things and focus on those. Paul and the sailors on the ship knew that they needed to get rid of a few things so they could reach shore. They let the clutter go. They even let go of the things that were purposeful at one time but now were weighing them down—and they focused on the main thing. Don't let the waves crashing against you distract you from your priorities. Make decisions that honor God, commit to loving God and people, create a good conscience, and build a sincere faith. Remember you are headed to your shore. Resisting the temptation to be distracted with the temporary and keeping focused on the right things will help you get there.

By the way . . . if your house caught on fire and you could save only three things, what would they be?

Get Your Hopes Up

Life is not the way it's supposed to be.
It's the way it is. The way you deal with
it is what makes the difference.

—Virginia Satir

Everything can be taken from a man
but one thing: the last of the human
freedoms—to choose one's attitude in
any given set of circumstances.

—Viktor Frankl

As a pastor and teacher, I find it is easier to preach a message about getting through hard times than it is to actually do it. This past year was a tough one for me. The storms were relentless, one after another after another. My father passed away suddenly. He loved me well, and he demonstrated that love every day of my life. I know my dad is in heaven, and I remind myself often about the truth that Jesus went to prepare a place for all of us, my dad included.[1] But I miss him every day.

Just a month after my dad died, someone hacked into Philip's and my personal accounts and stole thousands of dollars. We still haven't gotten that money back. Such a painful, time-consuming, distracting storm.

We had long conversations with the police and the FBI and all to no avail. The money is gone, and the feeling of vulnerability remains.

As if those storms weren't harsh enough, I experienced a couple of knee-buckling, backstabbing betrayals by some close friends. When I first discovered what had happened, I was shocked, then I wanted to hurt back. Then I just cried for days. Eventually I got to the truth of forgiveness. I felt God whisper that I was not only to forgive but actually act toward them as if they were already forgiven. I know this is God's way, His truth, but the fact is, forgiving is hard to do.

And then my marriage took a hit. Philip and I live together, work together, and play together. Lots of together. And this year, we just got on each other's nerves. As storm after storm crashed against us, too often we forgot we were on the same boat.

And finally to top off my banner year, Philip was diagnosed with lymphoma. The doctor assured us that this type of lymphoma was curable, and so within a few months Philip began treatment. The chemo left him weak and his immune system vulnerable. A few weeks after he finished his medical care, he got shingles. Sigh. He was in such pain that he could not move for weeks—he was basically out of commission for months. Such a tough storm.

Even though that year is technically over, I know the storms aren't. I can still feel waves crashing against my heart and my life. I don't tell you about all these storms because I want your pity. I just want you to know that you are not alone in your storms. I am working to put into practice all that I'm sharing in this book. It is much easier to preach it than to practice it, but in this moment I am doing my best to do both.

Hope is what sustained me this year. Hope that it would get better. Hope for a better tomorrow is what allowed me to get up another day and take another step. And I discovered that hope shines brightest in the middle of midnight storms. So how do we get our hopes up when waves continue to crash against us?

CHEER UP! AND THAT'S NO PLATITUDE

In the middle of a storm, most of us want to panic. We are racked with worry and weighed down with hopelessness. Paul saw these symptoms in the sailors as their ship was being tossed around on the sea. The crew started to panic and Paul told them to cheer up. He let them know that God would do what He promised—and He promised that none of their lives would be lost, that they would all get to shore.

> Cheer up! I am sure that God will
> do exactly what he promised.
>
> —Acts 27:25, CEV

Paul had a visit from an angel, who reassured him that he would indeed get to Rome to stand before Caesar. The angel also told him that the ship would be destroyed but that all lives would be saved. So Paul encouraged the men with the angel's words. God promised they would make it through this storm.[2] Sometimes that is all we need to hear. So let me tell you: you will make it through.

Unlike Paul, I have gotten in trouble when I have told someone in the midst of a storm to "cheer up." Actually it can be dangerous. As Philip was spending his fourth week in bed, I may have uttered those words. Not smart. And honestly, I'm not sure I want to hear them either—not when I am struggling through a difficult situation. Paul challenged us to "rejoice with those who rejoice; mourn with those who mourn."[3] The reason Paul could tell the sailors to cheer up is because he was in the middle of the storm with them. He was not an outsider looking in. So before we tell someone to cheer up, maybe we should share in that person's grief. We should be great at listening and understanding someone else's pain. And since I am in the middle of the storm with you, can I encourage you? Maybe I can't go straight to "Cheer up!" But how about "Get your hopes up!"? God is faithful. He was faithful with His promise to Paul, and He will keep His Word to you.

HOPE IS ESSENTIAL FOR THE JOURNEY

A few years ago, Philip and I toured the ancient catacombs of Rome where thousands of early Christians are buried. As an expression of faith, when a believer died, a Christian symbol was carved into the marble tombstone. Hundreds of different symbols line the walls: a fish, a shepherd, an anchor. Maybe the anchor was inspired by Hebrews 6:19: "We have this hope as an anchor for the soul, firm and secure."

What hope was the author talking about?

The firm expectation that the God who began this work in me will finish it.

Jesus told us that in this world we would have tough times, but in the next breath, He promised that we should be of good cheer because He has overcome the world.[4] Yes, you will encounter storms, but you can have hope because He will see you through!

I have heard that people can live about forty days without food, three days without water, and eight minutes without air. But they can live only one second without hope. Hope is more than optimism. In the New Testament, the biblical definition of hope implies a knowing, a sure expectation. When hopelessness fills your heart, death begins to take over—death to your dreams, to a relationship worth saving, to the idea that things will get better. The power of hope coursing through your veins can be your most valuable asset because it creates a tremendous force within you. Hope is not a luxury; it is an essential. Hope can change tragedy to opportunity, dreaded work to exciting, worthwhile effort, and weariness to invincibility.

Hope is for all of us. Not just those "glass half full" people. Hope is not wishing; it is not positive thinking. It *is* a sure expectation that God will do what He promised. Hope is like floaties. Have you seen children in a pool wearing those little flotation armbands in order to keep their heads above the water? Hope is like that. It keeps you floating until you get to solid ground.

I have a friend who suffers from an eating disorder. Many people told her that she might get help for a moment, but that the disorder would be a continual battle for her. She was floundering in this storm. When I spoke with her, I assured her that there would come a day in which this issue would no longer be her struggle. She could find freedom. I told her stories of many women who have wrestled with this challenge and are now free. They did the work of dealing with issues in their soul, allowed the Holy Spirit to bring transformation, and are now completely on the other side of it. Healed. I reminded her that the same God who started a work in her would finish it. I reminded her of her value. In a sense, my words, "Cheer up!"—and more importantly, God's words—gave her floaties. Hope was born in her and enabled her to continue her swim toward shore.

What are you in the middle of that hope seems lost?

Maybe you have lost your job.

Or your husband had an affair.

Or you can't seem to kick that addiction.

Or your child continues to struggle at school.

Or you hear the word *cancer* from your doctor.

Or you feel stuck in a dead-end job.

Or you wonder if the secret dream in your heart will ever come to pass.

How is hope possible? The Old Testament prophet Jeremiah has an answer:

I'll never forget the trouble, the utter lostness,
    the taste of ashes, the poison I've swallowed.

I remember it all—oh, how well I remember—
    the feeling of hitting the bottom.
But there's one other thing I remember,
    and remembering, *I keep a grip on hope:*

GOD's loyal love couldn't have run out,
    his merciful love couldn't have dried up.
They're created new every morning.
    How great your faithfulness!
I'm sticking with GOD (I say it over and over).
    He's all I've got left.[5]

Sometimes the bravest thing you can do is to keep hoping, and oftentimes, to keep a grip on hope will take both hands. Where are you drowning? Put on those floaties. You are being made stronger with every wave, and this storm is not bigger than the God who dwells in you. His name is Immanuel—God With Us.

As wave after wave crashed against my life this year, my hope came as I remembered that He is with me in every wave. He is not the aloof God up in heaven watching from a distance as His people suffer. No. He is *with* me. He is *with* you. In every moment. He sees and collects every tear (and I cried a lot of them).[6]

At one time King David cried so much that he soaked his pillows with tears. In fact, Psalm 6 is a great one to meditate on while you are in the midst of the storm. David began the psalm with complaints and expressed his hurts. He was dealing with sickness, trouble in his mind, and enemies who wanted to take him out. He was experiencing stormy wave after stormy wave. He ended this short psalm acknowledging that God heard his cries and received his prayer. His hope came from knowing that he was not in this alone.

Neither are you. It might feel overwhelming right now. Totally understandable. With God's help and a renewed perspective, you will get through this, and ultimately you will even help others navigate their storms.

I have a friend whose teenage daughter was tragically killed in an accident. She told me that one way she got through the agony of the days and weeks after the funeral was the hope that one day she could help someone else. That is amazing hope. And it's available for us too.

HOPE FLOATS

As we grasp what hope is and how important it is for our safely navigating a storm, we can then have more power over the other things that come into our lives—such as out-of-control emotions. (Never fear, we'll talk a lot about emotions throughout this book!) Too many of us make decisions based on how we feel—and that can lead us into more pain. But there's good news: we have more control over our emotions and attitudes than we may realize, thanks to the hope we hold within us. Our circumstances do not determine our attitude; neither do other people. So many times this past year I wanted to blame others for how bad I was feeling, but at the end of the day, I had to take control over my own thoughts, decisions, and emotions. It is possible!

We read many times in the psalms that when David was at a low point, he told his soul (his mind, will, and emotions) to rejoice. One time while David and some of his men were away, David's camp was destroyed and his family as well as the families of his men were kidnapped. When he came upon the scene, he began to cry. Sobbed. I imagine the situation looked hopeless. Then he began to worship God. He took control of his soul and worshiped; his emotions were no longer leading him. Now he could hear from God and take the next step.[7]

I doubt David felt like praising God. Yet, as he had many times before, he told his soul to praise God.[8] When all hell is breaking loose in my life, I never feel like worshiping God. I want to keep on crying. I want to be angry. I want to hurt someone. It is okay to cry; it is okay to be angry.

It is not okay to hurt someone. We are not robots who don't feel; we just can't let our emotions lead us. If I let those emotions run loose, I will not make it out of the storm.

Years ago my daughter flirted with making a bad decision, one that would have had serious consequences. It is her story to tell, and I am sure she will tell it one day. But from my side, I began to freak out. I cried more than I ever have. I had no idea how to deal with the situation, and it felt like I was drowning. So I did what I have told you to do. I opened my Bible and spoke the truth of His Word over my daughter. Isaiah 44:3–5 tells me that God will pour His spirit and blessing upon my daughter. She will rise and say, "I belong to the LORD." Every time my mind started to panic, I spoke the truth.

Then I called someone who had navigated a similar situation, and she reminded me God was with me. I braced my life by speaking the Word of God, and I let the encouragement of a friend soothe me. I chose to hold on to hope knowing that this was merely a season, not the end of the story. Keeping that tight grip on hope, I took hold of my runaway emotions and commanded my soul to worship God. Again, I did not feel like it. I just wasn't going to let my emotions take me down a path from which it would be hard to recover. I put on my floaties and found my brave.

So how about you? Are you in a situation where your emotions are taking over? What verse in the Bible can you hold on to?

WHAT HOPE PRODUCES IN US

To use another metaphor, wouldn't it be great if life were one mountaintop experience after another? Mountaintop . . . mountaintop . . . mountaintop . . . heaven. It is easy to believe God is on our side when so much good stuff happens. It is easy to have hope when we are on the mountaintop. But the truth is, every mountain has a valley. And I have learned that fruit does not grow on the mountaintops—fruit grows in the valleys.

Mount Conness and Cathedral Peak are just two mountains among the many that make up the Sierra Nevada range in California. The view is spectacular from their peaks, but there is no fruit there. California's Central Valley is located at the base of this mountain range, and it yields a third of all produce grown in the United States.[9] In most cases it is watered by the runoff from the mountains that surround it.

So just a thought. Jesus calls Himself the "living water,"[10] and maybe it is the living water that runs down our lives from our mountaintop encounters with Him that keeps us strong and grows our character in the valleys of life.

The fruit of our lives—love, joy, kindness, gentleness, patience— grows in the valleys of life. Paul told us that we can "glory in our sufferings, because we know that suffering produces perseverance; perseverance, character; and character, hope." Then he reminded us that "hope does not put us to shame, because God's love has been poured out into our hearts through the Holy Spirit who has been given to us."[11] And this is the reason Paul told the sailors, and us, to cheer up. God is with us, and these storms are not only producing character in us but also hope.

While Jesus told us that we would encounter trials, distress, and frustration between here and our ultimate, eternal shore, He also said He has "deprived [the world] of power to harm [us]"[12] and knock us off course. The mountaintop experiences are awesome, and I hope you have lots and lots of them, and at the same time I do know that you will be made stronger in the valleys.

WE HOPE BECAUSE WE FIGHT FROM A PLACE OF VICTORY

I like confetti. Being in a room when confetti cannons are launched makes me smile. How can you not laugh in the midst of a confetti storm? (Unless you are the one who has to clean it up.) One of my favorite Bible verses says, "In Christ, God leads us from place to place in one perpetual victory parade."[13] About it, in one of my previous books, I wrote,

> Paul was referring to the victory parade Caesar gave when one of his Roman generals succeeded in a military campaign. In this parade there was dancing, music, and cheering (and, I am sure, confetti!). The conquering general rode in a great chariot pulled by white horses, and his army followed. They all shared in the glory of the celebration Caesar threw on behalf of the military leader. What an awesome sight it must have been! The picture for you and me is this: Jesus is our conquering General. You and I are part of His army . . . and share in the victory. He leads us in one perpetual victory parade.[14]

We need to see ourselves riding in the parade, cheering crowds lining the streets. You and I might be in the middle of a terrible storm, but we are not trudging through a world of misery. It might feel like it in this moment, but because of what Jesus did for us through His death and resurrection, we are in nothing less than a victory celebration! I believe this Scripture says not that we are fighting *for victory* but that we are fighting *from a place of victory.* In the darkest moments of our storms, when we can't see how this could possibly turn out well, we cling to our hope in Christ that brings us back to the place where we can remember that we are victorious. And that allows us to cheer up, as Paul encouraged the sailors to do!

Jesus paid a great price for us to walk in this parade—to live out a life of hope. God's intention, no matter what challenge we face, is for us to overcome. He is the God of storms. And He is the God who produces fruit from the valleys. Never lose sight of that!

And contrary to what others might say, go ahead and find your brave by putting on those floaties and getting your hopes up.

Courage Is a Decision

Promise me you'll always remember:
You're braver than you believe, and
stronger than you seem, and smarter
than you think.

—A. A. Milne

Fall seven times. Stand up eight.

—Proverbs 24:16 (my version)

A few years ago, during her last year of high school, my daughter, Paris, decided to run cross-country. Each race is about five kilometers and takes place on challenging trails: over obstacles, up hills, and through the brush. While she runs, I have a different experience. I have no refs to yell at, no stands to sit in, and no place to watch the entire race. When she first started, I was sure I'd find it boring. Boy, was I wrong! In one race, Paris was elbowed in the stomach as she was running. In another race, she threw up as she crossed the finish line. And then there was the race where she was crying as she crossed the finish line.

"I have to get help!" she told me, gasping for breath.

My mama's heart panicked. That did it: *No more running for her!* I thought. But she explained that as she had been running on a fairly remote part of the trail, she came upon another runner who had fallen. Paris stopped to check on her. The girl had hit her head and wasn't moving.

When Paris asked if she was okay, the girl whispered, "Why are you stopping? You aren't on my team."

Before Paris could reply another runner approached, jumped over the hurt girl, and continued on her way. Paris couldn't believe she had done that. She reassured the hurt girl, "It doesn't matter whose team you're on. We are all runners." Then Paris helped the girl up and walked her up the hill.

Soon Paris's coach saw Paris and the injured girl; he went down the hill to see what was going on. He told Paris to run for the finish line and to send help since this girl was seriously injured. So Paris started running again, finished her race, told me, and we got help. Eventually an ambulance came to take the girl to the hospital.

You just never know what might happen in a race. All the runners begin at the starting line. Ready, full of hope, with visions of the finish line, they take off. They must navigate the curves, the hills, the heat. They must occasionally take a punch in the stomach and perhaps stop to help a fallen runner. The runners will encounter lots of challenges in their race toward their finish.

Cross-country running is like life. We step up to the starting line, full of hope and dreams . . . and then the race starts. We must navigate the curves of life: heat, challenges, loss, heartbreak, fallen sisters . . . and the occasional punch in the stomach. As we run toward our finish line, we realize that life is not a pain-free, risk-free ride. We may panic and decide we don't want to run this course anymore.

We need courage. That something in our gut that lets us know that even though the Enemy might be messing with us, the Spirit of God is stirring within—building true bravery.

What Courage Really Looks Like

Many of us associate bravery with big, dangerous actions, such as facing an enemy on a battlefield or accomplishing an amazing feat of physical strength, like lifting a car off a trapped victim. Others might associate courage with doing something spectacular, such as skydiving or climbing Mount Everest.

And while all those feats take courage, it's important to remember that bravery is not limited to the impressive actions of a few. When God asks you to be brave, He is talking about the everyday, ordinary moments of bravery. Real bravery is finishing the race even if you are in last place. It is standing up to your daughter when she wants to go out with the boy who is "cool" but dangerous. Bravery is having an honest talk with your children about the mistakes of your past so they won't go down those same roads. Bravery is forgiving your friend when she lets you down. It is loving your husband in the midst of a financial crisis. Finding your brave is telling the truth or asking for help or loving someone difficult to love. It is applying for that job or not going to that party or . . . not sleeping with that guy.

Finding your brave is taking that first step out of your comfort zone, which is hard to do, because our comfort zone is, well, *comfortable* . . . and we like comfort.

The children of Israel learned this important lesson after they had wandered in the desert for forty years, waiting to enter the Promised Land. After so many years, they had grown comfortable with their situation. They may not have liked it, but they were used to it. Then God called them to find their brave and take the land He had prepared for them: "Moses my servant is dead. Therefore, the time has come for [Joshua] to lead these people, the Israelites, across the Jordan River into the land I am giving them."[1]

I imagine this announcement produced mixed emotions: grief

because their fearless leader was dead; excitement because now was the time to step into the land of promise; and fear, because they were going to face new challenges. They knew the ground before them was filled with enemies who wanted to kill them! Literally. As they looked at what lay ahead, I'm sure many of them thought the wilderness was not such a bad place to be after all. It was better than the slavery in Egypt they had come from. But the desert they'd wandered in was not the Promised Land.

It's the same for us. God's plan for us, as it was for the Israelites, is strength-to-strength, glory-to-glory walking in courage.[2]

COURAGE BEYOND THE STORM

Paul understood this idea of stepping out into bravery. Granted, being in the middle of a storm isn't comfortable, but it's easier to withdraw than it is to step out of our comfort zone of fear. As Paul's ship navigated stormy conditions day after day, he encouraged the sailors to find their brave.

So take courage! For I believe God.
It will be just as he said.

—Acts 27:25, NLT

They were in the middle of blustery conditions beyond their control, but courage was within reach. Paul reminded the sailors on the ship, and us, that if we are going to reach our shore, we must make the decision to stand brave. We can't control the circumstances we face, but just as we can control how we think about them, we can also control how we approach them.

It wasn't just that Paul bravely faced the storm; it was also that Paul was able to look beyond the storm. That's courage—but it isn't the courage that we have on our own. It comes from trusting God; it comes from the Holy Spirit who provides courage in those moments of fear. Paul understood that, and so he was able to encourage his fellow shipmates to be brave as well: "I believe God. It will be just as he said." In other words, it wasn't just about getting safely to shore—it was also about what Paul was called to do once on that shore.

It's the same for us. Our ordinary moments of bravery may not be as glamorous as those of the skydiving friend or the hero who stands up to a gunman, but they have far greater impact. Jesus's bravery in the Garden of Gethsemane when He said, "Not my will, but yours be done,"[3] set the standard. He knew the path ahead, while ultimately ending in victory, would definitely involve pain and hardship. His bravery opened the door for all of us to look beyond the storm.

BRAVE WOMEN RUN IN OUR FAMILY

We come from a long line of believers who found their brave. When our Hebrew ancestors spoke of freedom, they spoke of uncharted territory, not as a threat but as an opportunity to be led into the heart of God. If we follow in their footsteps, we forfeit an easy life and sacrifice everything to make the lives of those who follow us free as well.

When fear tries to direct our journey, we can resist, knowing that our DNA is encrypted with an aversion to settling. Remember this: settling never made it into the plot line of our family tree.

Courage did.

There was an orphan who found herself in a queen's quarters. Her uncle's faith presented her with a life-or-death decision. She had to choose between her own safety and her people's existence. Esther chose courage, and a nation was saved.

Safety never motivates a courageous woman anyway. It is the heart, and all that it begs of us, that motivates our steps. To follow it, and everything God has placed within us, requires surrender of temporary comfort and a desire for eternal freedom.

Another woman was a virgin whose plan for a comfortable life took a detour when she chose God's plan over her own, despite the shame and humiliation. Because Mary chose to follow God into the storm, our freedom was born.

Sometimes what starts out as a small act of bravery snowballs into something that changes many lives. A woman named Thecla was the most famous missionary of her day. She initially heard the gospel during Paul's first missionary journey to Asia Minor. She was so inspired by the gospel that she ended her engagement and rejected her family's wealth in order to become a follower of Christ. Enraged at her decision, her parents attempted to have her raped, burned, and thrown to wild animals. She miraculously escaped all of these. She found her brave and courageously gave up all the comforts of her upper-class lifestyle in order to serve as a missionary near Antioch, where she had a vibrant ministry. Years later, church fathers Basil and Gregory spoke of her ministry in Syria as a center of teaching and healing. In 1906, archeologists in Ephesus discovered a fresco of Thecla seated next to Paul, indicating that her leadership in the early church was well known. And in 1908, German archeologists excavated her hospital, saying it was the size of a football field.[4]

Now let's fast forward a bit.

In 1820, Harriet Tubman was born into slavery and treated brutally, yet she escaped to Philadelphia when she was in her late twenties. She could have remained safe in her comfortable life in Philadelphia, but instead she returned to the South, time and time again, helping to rescue slaves. She was not looking for the safe life, but rather she trusted that her safest place was with her hand in the hand of her God. She did not intend to shape history, yet she helped to rescue more than three hundred slaves. Her simple belief that enough was enough awoke the conscience of a country; when she found her brave, others found freedom.

Gladys Aylward was just an everyday woman who at the age of twenty-six gave up a life of comfort and immigrated to China. She risked her life to demonstrate the love of God to the Chinese who had never heard of this Jesus. She helped with prison reform, took in orphans, protected young girls from the tortuous process of foot binding, and during the Japanese invasion of 1940, led more than one hundred orphans to freedom.[5] She found her brave.

Corrie ten Boom lived in the Netherlands with her family. They were devoted in their faith and committed to serving their community. In the midst of German occupation and persecution of the Jews in the early 1940s, Corrie risked her life to protect them, ultimately saving as many as eight hundred. She and her family were eventually sent to a concentration camp where her sister was killed. Corrie was just an ordinary woman who found her brave and was willing to stand up for others in the face of injustice.

When we read or hear about these women, we call them heroes. And they are. But first they were everyday ordinary women like you and me. Each woman simply made a decision to step out of her comfort zone and not let difficult circumstances crush her. Each of these women faced fear and risked retaliation. They looked beyond their circumstances and listened to the Holy Spirit to take the next step of courage.

These amazing women have shown us that we can find our brave. So don't imprison yourself in your comfort zone. (Even storms can have aspects of a comfort zone, can't they?) Have the courage to step out of your comfort zone and take the first step into the unknown.

GOD IS OUR PERSONAL BRAVERY

The prophet Habakkuk calls God our personal bravery. He is *my* bravery. It is not just some ethereal concept of bravery, but one that is real and personal.

> The Lord God is my Strength, *my personal bravery,* and my
> invincible army; He makes my feet like hinds' feet and will make
> me to walk [not to stand still in terror, but to walk] and make

[spiritual] progress upon my high places [of trouble, suffering, or responsibility]![6]

This last year, time and again, I read this verse to remind myself that I can be strong, make good decisions, and keep taking the next step.

I believe I have been sent to the planet at this time in history to fulfill a plan of God's. My life is not my own. It is His. And He will help me in every storm because . . .

He is my personal bravery.

He is my invincible army.

And because He is both of those, He will cause me to walk—not stand still in terror, but *walk*. Which means I can't allow myself to get overwhelmed with whatever obstacle might be in front of me on the path of my God-mission, on my journey to shore.

Because He is my bravery. Personally. Mine. And He is yours too.

Your journey to your shore may include taking care of aging parents or special-needs children or enduring a marriage that is hanging on by dental floss.

You may be facing a battery of medical tests.

You may be handling staggering financial challenges.

You may have lost a job.

You may not be able to find a job.

You may have had your heart broken.

You may have lost a loved one.

You just may not know the next step to take.

That's why we need courage. We need God-sized bravery. Actually, we have something even better than God-sized bravery. God Himself is our courage.

I spoke recently with a young woman whose husband had a stroke and she herself is dealing with a painful sickness.

Another young woman told me that her parents' marriage of twenty-five years was ending. She felt lost and confused.

Whatever the challenge, He is our personal bravery. And when He *is* our strength and bravery, then He will make us walk—not freak out, but walk. And not only walk, but also make progress in our areas of trouble and suffering. If that is you right now, just breathe. He is your bravery.

We remain confident because He is our bravery. He will also cause us to make progress in our areas of responsibility.

I love that Habakkuk uses the word *responsibility*. Not a glamorous word, but somehow reassuring.

You may get up day after day and go to the same job and do the same thing.

You may daily take care of children and wonder if you will ever again have an adult conversation.

You may go to school every day and wonder where it will lead.

You may wake up and look at the same man that you have been looking at for the last twenty-five years.

You may be paying all of your own bills for the first time and wonder if being an adult is worth it.

All these seemingly not grand moments demand responsibility.

As you and I live out life in the places where consistency, reliability, and dependability are demanded of us, those too call us to find our brave. And God will meet us there. He will help us so that we can make progress, not only in the big areas of challenge and suffering but also in the daily, mundane, possibly boring areas of responsibility. He is with us and He is for us. Whatever we face—trouble, suffering, or the everydayness of responsibility—He is our personal bravery.

When I think of the story of Joshua in light of God being our personal bravery, I think of God telling Joshua, and us, "Haven't I commanded you? Strength! Courage! Don't be timid; don't get discouraged. GOD, your God, is with you every step you take."[7]

He is with us and that is why we can take courage.

After Moses's death, and even though he might have doubted his qualifications, Joshua took over leading the children of Israel. At God's word, he realized he was the one to lead them into the Promised Land. Maybe you doubt your qualifications. But He is your personal bravery. He is with you.

Our courage in everyday life, no matter our circumstances, glorifies God because there is no way we could be brave without Him. I don't know about you, but like Joshua, I face many situations where I am confident I don't have what it takes. But with my hope in God, with my trust in Him, He will make me brave as I step out in obedience to Him.

OTHER REASONS WE CAN CHOOSE COURAGE

With God as our personal bravery, there are a few more reasons we can be brave.

First, I know who I am. I am the loved-beyond-measure daughter of the King. My father is the God of the Angel Armies, Creator of the Universe, Lover of My Soul, and my identity is found as I focus on Him. The same is true for you.

Second, we can be brave because we know that heaven is our home. As followers of Jesus, we are citizens of another world. This world is our assignment but not our home. We will never be fully comfortable here. Our purpose is eternal. Paul wrote us that "our citizenship is in heaven,"[8] that we are seated with Christ in heavenly places,[9] and that we are "Christ's ambassadors."[10]

As ambassadors we live in one world while we represent another. Our job here on earth is to represent the heart of God and to fulfill His mission. All of God's resources, including His angelic army, are at our disposal as we carry out the King's orders. We are brave not because of our name but because we are here with the full support of heaven's armies when we are on a mission with Him.

Third, we can be brave because "God causes everything to work together for the good of those who love God and are called according to his purpose for them. For God knew his people in advance, and he chose them to become like his Son."[11] All things. Every wave. Every storm.

When the storms and waves crash against your boat, cling to this promise that He is using all things to work together for your good as He is forming you into the image of His Son.

When Paul was in the midst of that storm, he knew they were headed toward shore, and that is why he could say, "Take courage!"

Find your brave. Keep looking forward. This storm will not last forever.

WE CHOOSE COURAGE BECAUSE OF WHO WE ARE

In his letter to the church at Ephesus, Paul refers to us as "God's master-piece."[12] His work of art. I don't always feel like I am His masterpiece, His tapestry, but I am. So are you. The thing is, God works from the backside of the tapestry. You may have heard this illustration before, but stick with me. Over the years I have watched my mom do needlework, and I have noticed that the back of the canvas looks nothing like what is being produced on the front. The back looks like an absolute mess. Most of the time I cannot see the pattern. It is the same with our lives.

As God works from the backside, He will use all the threads—those that come from bad choices, those that come from life, and those that come from the Enemy. We may not see a pattern. Instead it just looks like a tangled mess of threads and knots and a mismatched grouping of colors, but He will take them all and form us into His masterpiece—because we love Him and are called according to His purpose.

You might not like the color of the thread. Perhaps this dark thread in your tapestry is the thread that came when your spouse left you or when you lost your job, or maybe it represents a season of waiting and not seeing an answer. Of course you are hurt and angry, but if you let God, He will make all things work together for good.

You might say, "Yes, but how?"

To be honest, I don't know.

I don't know how He makes my heart beat.

I don't know how He keeps the planets in orbit.

I don't know how a seed becomes a tree.

I don't know how a man's brain works.

I don't know.

But I do know that all things work together for good for those who love Him, who are surrendered to Him. It is a mystery of His grace, but I can find my brave because I know that He is worthy of my trust. From my perspective on the tapestry of my life, all I can see are the bits and pieces because I am constrained by time. The lens I see with is temporal, but His view is eternal.

When I think of all Paul went through as he followed Jesus, it is staggering. He wrote many of his magnificent letters while in prison. I would imagine that he didn't like those particular threads of his tapestry. I'm sure he was frustrated and wanted to be outside those walls and doing something for Jesus. Yet there he was stuck in prison. But now, it is those large portions of Scripture—Paul's letters—that have shaped our theology and helped frame the church.

Paul suffered many things, yet in his letter to the Corinthian church, he referred to what he suffered as "light affliction" in relation to the big picture. Do you know what he considered "light affliction"?[13]

Being betrayed.

Being whipped.

Being beaten with rods.

Being shipwrecked.

Being bitten by a poisonous snake.[14]

These are pretty bad threads! At one point he prayed that he would have sufficient courage.[15] And he did. Which is why he can say to us with confidence, "Take courage!"

We can learn a lot from the way Paul showed courage and believed that God was his personal bravery. God has a plan for history and a plan for your life. Let me say that again: God has a divine plan for history and a divine plan for your life. Sometimes we just have trouble seeing the other side of the tapestry because we get trapped in our view of the tangled mess of threads. Will you choose courage, trusting that He is using all the threads of your life to form you into the image of Jesus?

Just to be clear, it is not good when bad things happen. It is not good when divorce comes, betrayal wounds a heart, a friend dies, or cancer strikes. This "all things work together for good" verse is not a panacea that we are to quote to people who are in the midst of devastation. But in the midst of all that pain, we move from quoting the verse to knowing it.

I know it can be hard to believe. Because we see our flaws. We know our failures. How can the tragedies and mistakes of life turn into anything good? And yet "we *know* that in all things God works for the good of those who love him, who have been called according to his purpose."[16]

We get impatient as we wait for Him to make all things good. In the verses right before that promise, Paul assures us that God's Spirit is working in us and with us: "Meanwhile, the moment we get tired in the waiting, God's Spirit is right alongside helping us along."[17]

We have to let the Holy Spirit in, allowing Him to help us in our weaknesses.

Can we believe He is our personal bravery, even if a particular situation doesn't go the way we want it to go? When I was dealing with cancer, I knew I was going to be healed. I was going to be healed through the wisdom of doctors, miraculously by God, or in heaven if I died. He is working all things together for good. We need to be brave, whatever the circumstances, because Jesus is our eternal hope and His story is eternal good.

In a few places in Psalms, it tells us that God is good and He does good.

You are good, and what you do is good. (119:68)

Give thanks to the LORD, for he is good. (136:1)

Because that is true, can we choose to trust when we don't understand?

We see only with our finite minds; we have only a temporal perspective. Sometimes we just get stuck on the backside of the tapestry, but our
story is being written beyond our last breath here. God is positioning us
for what He is doing on the earth. He sees you and knows where you
are. Paul reminded us, "We all, who with unveiled faces contemplate the
Lord's glory, *are being transformed into his image with ever-increasing
glory,* which comes from the Lord, who is the Spirit."[18]

During dark, gloomy, and often brutal times, God has always had a
person He could use to declare truth and fight on His behalf. Today there
is much darkness. And since God always has a person, a people to further
His purpose, let's be those people. Let's remain faithful—even in the
storm. Take courage. Let's find our brave and be people He can trust.
Let's believe that He is creating the tapestry of our lives and that all things
will work together for good. Our good. His good. With every thread, we
are being formed into His image to bring His Spirit to a culture that so
desperately needs to see Jesus.

Not Holly.

But Jesus.

Not you.

But Jesus.

Anchored

All you need is one safe anchor to keep
you grounded when the rest of your life
spins out of control.

—Katie Kacvinsky

Contentment is not the fulfillment of
what you want, but the realization of
how much you already have.

—Unknown

In the weeks after that 1994 earthquake, Philip and I got tired of our earth moving. During the first week post-earthquake, we experienced thousands of aftershocks. Freeways and apartment buildings near our home had collapsed, killing dozens of people and causing more than twenty billion dollars worth of damage.[1]

We thought, *Hey, let's move to a place in the country that doesn't shake!* We were still battling fear with every tremor. We didn't pray; we just thought, *Let's get out of here!*

It's embarrassing to admit that we actually visited different cities, looking for one we thought would be a good place to plant a church. We didn't tell anyone. We just wanted to escape the land of the San Andreas fault.

Ultimately, Philip and I came to our senses and stayed put. I cringe now to think of what we almost did. Not that there aren't other great places to plant a church; they just aren't other great places for us. Our calling lies in Los Angeles—earthquakes (gulp!) and all.

The feeling like you want to run is normal. Really. This last year as storm after storm hit my life, I kept thinking, *Is there any other place I can be? Is there a safe harbor somewhere that is immune to storms?* Dr. Robert Schuller understood that feeling and cautioned us against reacting—and doing something unwise:

> The most dangerous thing in the world is to make an irreversible
> negative decision during a brownout time. Don't sell your real
> estate because there is no electricity in the building. It's just a
> brownout, not a burnout. . . . Never make a negative decision in
> the low time. Never make your most important decisions when
> you are in your worst mood.[2]

Dr. Schuller's words resonated with me and challenged me as my earth continued to shake. I slowly realized that when the ground is shaking, it is *not* the time to make major life-changing decisions. I understand that feeling of needing to do something, *anything,* to fix the situation, but making irreversible decisions when your world is trembling can bring about a whole new set of problems.

There's Strength in Dropping an Anchor

As the storm raged around the ship carrying the apostle Paul, the crew realized they couldn't just throw things overboard. Now they needed to pitch something else that would keep them focused directly toward the shore.

The Bible tells us that the crew dropped four anchors from the stern. The goal was to keep the bow from swinging around and to prepare the ship to run ashore when it was light and they could find a suitable opportunity and place.[3] They wanted to keep the shore in front of them, so they dropped anchors.

They dropped four anchors from the stern and prayed for daylight.

—Acts 27:29

From the beginning of time on earth, God dignified humanity with the ability to choose. We are not puppets on a string, nor is God a bully forcing us to do His will. We get to decide. However, every choice we make has consequences, and most of us don't seem to think of the long-term effects of choices we make during a crisis. Storms cause us to want to get out RIGHT NOW! But if we don't anchor—and do it in the right way—we will get into even more trouble and potentially lose our way. Making dramatic decisions just isn't the best thing to do while a storm is still raging, mainly because our emotions can be topsy-turvy. Sometimes the bravest thing to do is to drop those anchors and hold on, waiting for the light of daybreak.

Whatever storm you are in, now is the time to drop anchors and hang on. When wave after wave hits your boat, when your life is confronted with challenge after challenge and it seems as if you are scrounging around for a footing, and looking for something that will stop the assault, make decisions that bring stability. I don't know that we can stop the onslaught of the waves, but I do know we can take measures that will help steady our lives in the midst of the storm.

A man who worked for an oil company told me that when a storm would hit, the ships bringing supplies to the oil rigs in the open sea would get as close as they could to a harbor and drop anchors. He said, the bigger the waves, the more anchors they would let go. I am not sure how many anchors you should release, but here are four I do my best to drop when the seas get rough.

ANCHOR 1: IDENTITY

As the waves beat against you, remember who you are. Knowing who we are in God is the foundation of everything in our lives, and it is crucial in a storm. The Enemy will come at you with accusations and doubts; you will defeat those with the knowledge of who God says you are.

In the midst of their storm, the American colonial revolutionaries knew who they were. In 1776 they declared their identity:

> When in the Course of human Events, it becomes necessary for one People to dissolve the political bands which have connected them with another, and to assume among the powers of the earth, the separate and equal station to which the Laws of Nature and of Nature's God entitle them, a decent respect to the opinions of mankind requires that they should declare the causes which impel them to the separation.
>
> We hold these truths to be self-evident, that all men are created equal, that they are endowed by their Creator with certain unalienable Rights, that among these are Life, Liberty and the pursuit of Happiness.[4]

They separated themselves from who they used to be and declared who they were. So who are we, and where do we get our identity? We don't get it from our driver's license—most of the stuff on there is not true anyway! (Be honest, how much does yours say you weigh?) We don't get it from our passports—those just tell us where we've been. We don't get our identity from school report cards—most of us are still dealing with the negative things some teachers said.

You and I get our identity from our Creator. It's through our Creator's eyes that we get a true picture of who we are.

We are

- not victims, but conquerors—in fact, "more than conquerors"[5]
- not losers, but winners[6]
- not addicts, but overcomers[7]
- not captives, but free[8]
- not sinners, but forgiven[9]
- not random creations or our parents' "accident," but persons placed on the earth "for such a time as this"[10]

As a daughter of the King, I need to remember I have a crown on my head. I am royalty—not to be served, but to serve. All of that is who I am. And in the midst of the storm, I need to keep this in mind and drop that anchor, or I will lose my way.

I have written my own declaration. Not of independence, but of freedom.

> In the course of my life, it has become necessary to dissolve the bands that have tied me to my past and to assume the powers to which God has entitled me. I hold these truths to be self-evident: I have been created in the image of God and have bold access to Him at all times. I am His daughter and have all the privileges that come with royalty: I am forgiven, loved unconditionally, free from guilt and shame, healed, and destined for a life of purpose and blessing. I am set apart to bring life and joy to a hurting world, and I have the courage to do so!

A few years ago I talked with a woman who had been sober for eight years. As we spoke, I learned that her father had died just a few months ago, her engagement ended a few weeks later, and she'd spent the day before at the funeral of a good friend. Wave after wave of loss was crashing against her life. She looked at me with tears in her eyes and confessed, "I just want to drink again."

I understand wanting to numb the pain, I really do. And that is what I told her. I also told her that I was proud of her for coming and telling me. I prayed for her, hugged her, connected her with another young woman in our church, and began to remind her of who she is. She is slowly dropping the anchor of identity—reminding her soul that she is a valued daughter of the King. I could see the battle going on inside her. The battle to believe that she has value and that her life and decisions matter. That anchor is helping to hold her steady as she navigates the heartbreak. She found her brave.

As we talked about in chapter 2, when you declare the truth of God's Word over your life, it has the power to break every lie. As our thoughts change, our behavior changes and we begin to walk strong as the women our Creator made us to be. Know who you are in Him. Your ability to fight, to make it through the storm, comes when you do! Jesus said that if we don't have real roots, if we are not grounded, then when (not if, but when!) affliction or trouble or persecution comes, we will stumble.[11] We will stop trusting God and His plans for us.

I don't want to be one who stumbles through life, so I better make sure I know who and whose I am. I want the same for you.

ANCHOR 2: PURPOSE

When the winds are tossing us in every direction, we can easily lose our way if we don't understand that we were created for a reason. That sounds like such a big thing to know, but it really isn't that complicated. God created you and me for a reason. We are not here just to suck in air. We are not exploded tadpoles randomly placed on earth. No. We are the loved-beyond-measure daughters of the King, created to fulfill His plan for our life.

At the end of my life, I don't want people to say only that I paid all my bills on time, made a great peanut butter sandwich, and drove safely. Surely God put me here for more than that!

God's purpose for us doesn't change. As we grow and mature, the plan gets more refined, but it doesn't alter. Sometimes, however, in the midst of a storm, because our world is dark and chaotic, we make bad decisions that indicate we have forgotten why we are here.

A young woman I met a few years ago felt called to Los Angeles, specifically to the film industry. She came to take classes at a prestigious school in the city, and she was excited about the possibilities. At one point, she was struggling in school, and then a friend said some horrible things about her, which overwhelmed her with loneliness. As those waves crashed against her life, she decided to go to a club and find a guy. At the club she met a man, and they enjoyed one drink that led to another and another. She ended up going to that guy's apartment and sleeping with him. The next morning, he kicked her out. Months later she discovered she had an STD. For a moment one night, she had forgotten who she was and what she was on this earth to do. In the midst of the first storm, it would have been good for her to drop that purpose anchor. It may not initially have eased the school struggles or the loneliness, but it would have kept her from the club and the sex with a stranger.

As we discussed in chapter 4, we all have the same general purpose: to love God with everything we are, to worship Him, and to love our neighbors as ourselves. But the specifics of how we work that out are what make you and me unique.

Big picture: you are a daughter of the King, created to love God and lead people to Him.

Specifics: you may do that as a barista, grocery clerk, third-grade teacher, actor, musician, CEO, lawyer, student, pastor. And you'll do it while you are a single person, a teenager, a mom, a wife, a sister, a daughter, a friend, or a stay-at-home mom. Dropping the anchor of purpose means remembering that your assignment does not change no matter how big the waves are.

As a teenager, Philip knew he was supposed to be in ministry. That was the specific of his purpose. Like many of us, during his younger years, he experienced heartbreaks and financial hardships. In the midst of those storms, he looked for ways to ease the pain. He wasted years during his twenties smoking pot and partying. All that did was add more sorrow and bad relationship choices. Eventually he did find his brave, dropped the anchor of purpose, and once again headed down the path for which he was always created.

When we drop the anchor of purpose, it keeps us on track. It prevents us from drifting off course and reminds us of a future filled with possibilities. Anchors don't stop the storm; they just hold us steady as the waves continue to crash. Find your brave by remembering why you are here. Drop that anchor and hold on.

ANCHOR 3: CONTENTMENT

Contentment can be defined as resting in who you are and what you have. Today it might be rare to find someone who is truly content with his or her situation. Satisfaction isn't a matter of never trying to improve your situation; rather, it is just being at peace in this season.

Our lack of contentment springs from our *desire* for what we do not have. Author Lydia Brownback says, "We crave love, beauty, and comfort. We crave independence and peaceful surroundings. We crave self-esteem. We crave the smooth rhythm of a balanced life—a little of this, a bit of that, but not too much of either. We are unhappy because we have come to expect such things, living as we do in a society that advocates personal rights, autonomy, and prosperity above all else."[12] We've come to expect we can have it all whenever we want it.

The Bible has a great deal to say about contentment—resting in what we have, who we are, and where we're going. Jesus said, "Do not worry about your life, what you will eat or drink; or about your body, what you will wear. Is not life more than food, and the body more than clothes?"[13] In this context, He was mainly speaking to the everyday person and the marginalized, encouraging them not to compare themselves to those who seem to have it all. In this verse and those following, Jesus was telling them—and us—that anxiety was unnecessary and unprofitable. To underscore His point, He draws our attention to the birds of the air. They do not plow and plant, sow and reap, and store up provisions in barns, yet God provides for them. There is not a millionaire in the world who could afford to feed all the birds for just one day, but God never stops feeding them. We are of much more value than the birds. God cares for them and of course He cares for us.[14] The objects of our anxiety—food, drink, and clothing—are to be seen as less important than the *life* and the *body* that they supply. After that Jesus assures us that since God provides the latter, He can be trusted for the former.[15]

Basically Jesus is saying, "Be content." This is easier when life is good, when there is no storm to navigate, when we have all we need, when everyone likes us and everything is going our way. Remember those two times in your life when you had all you needed and everyone liked you and everything was going your way?! The challenge is to drop the anchor of contentment when the storm rages.

How? Well, contentment starts with gratitude. Paul tells us to "give thanks in all circumstances."[16] Not *for* all circumstances, but *in* them. I did not thank God for Philip's cancer, but I did worship Him in the middle of the journey. Often my worship was in the midst of tears. Sometimes it was on my knees. At times it was in frustration. Worship helped me find my brave and drop the anchor of contentment. I was not grateful for the heartbreaks of this last year, yet I did my best to celebrate God in the midst of them.

Contentment starts with gratitude, but really contentment is where

God is. In the midst of the storm, we can do our best to fight our way out of it, or we can invite God into the middle of it. I have found that when I put my longing for the presence and the wisdom of God first, then my other longings are satisfied, and contentment is within reach. This last year there were many times I walked around my backyard and worshiped God. I did not understand how I could get through the battles in front of me. All I knew was to ask Him to join me. Circumstances did not change immediately. Storms were still raging. I was just doing my best to drop that anchor of contentment in the middle of them.

And I found things to be grateful for. I have heard that if one has a roof over her head and a meal on her table, she is richer than more than 90 percent of the world's population. Do you have a roof over your head? Did you eat today? Then maybe we can start there and be thankful. Being grateful in this moment can help us to be content as the storm rages.

I certainly hoped for and longed for an end to this past year of relentless storms, but if I kept my focus solely at what I hoped tomorrow might bring, then I would miss whatever good today brings. Life is made up of todays, not tomorrows. What do you have today? Right now. In the midst of this storm. A good friend? A freshly baked chocolate chip cookie? Sunshine? Coffee?

The apostle Paul put it this way, "I've learned by now to be quite content whatever my circumstances. I'm just as happy with little as with much, with much as with little. I've found the recipe for being happy whether full or hungry, hands full or hands empty. Whatever I have, wherever I am, I can make it through anything in the One who makes me who I am."[17] This is the man who suffered imprisonment, beatings, and shipwrecks, and he said he had learned to be content in the middle of them. Whether he had a lot or a little, whether things went his way or not, he figured out how to be content. If he learned, we can too.

Right before Paul said that he had learned to be content, he shared one of the secrets that made that possible: he told us what he filled his mind with, and he challenged those of us looking for contentment to do the same.

> I'd say you'll do best by filling your minds and meditating on things true, noble, reputable, authentic, compelling, gracious— the best, not the worst; the beautiful, not the ugly; things to praise, not things to curse. Put into practice what you learned from me, what you heard and saw and realized. Do that, and God, who makes everything work together, will work you into his most excellent harmonies.[18]

Paul was telling us what to think about. Contentment comes by being grateful and by controlling our thoughts. Hold that thought! To drop that anchor of contentment means that our minds need to be meditating on the best, not the worst. That takes work. Real work. There were times this last year when I would start thinking about someone's hurtful words to me, and then I would keep reliving the pain. I would meditate on what they said over and over, and soon I would find myself depressed and hurting. Just with the focus of my thoughts, I had carved a rut I couldn't get out of. It took real discipline for me to begin to change my thoughts, to start meditating on things beautiful and gracious. And slowly contentment came.

ANCHOR 4: CHURCH HOME

I love the house of God. I think it should be the most creative, energetic, loving, awesome place on the earth. So does God. Yes, it is full of imperfect people on a journey (Hello? I am there . . . and so are you!), but it should be our number one destination when any storm hits. It is the vehicle God uses to establish His kingdom of love on the earth. As Paul declares, "the church of the living God" is "the pillar and foundation of the truth."[19]

Maybe you have encountered, instead of unconditional love, judgment and criticism in the house of God. I am sorry. For years a banner hanging in the lobby of our church read "Welcome Home," because we honestly want it to be a place where the lost, confused, and hurting come in and get help. Home should be a place where you recover and find refreshment.

In my years of leading in church, I have seen that when people are in storms, too often they run from church rather than to it. Maybe they are embarrassed that they are experiencing such deep difficulty, which is sad, because we all go through hard times. The house of God should be the first place someone goes when she hurts.

You and I are the church. My friend Bobbie Houston says,

> The Church is definitely not a building, but when we (flesh and blood) gather to the building, the building suddenly becomes 'the House of God.' When we leave and the lights go out, it is merely a building again. . . . This House has the capacity to be magnificent, wonderful, and awesome. It has the capacity to carry an anointing from above that can fulfill all of His purposes in all of our lives and it has the capacity to make a difference in the world. . . .
>
> So many churches and Christians fall short of their potential because they allow themselves to have a *casual relationship* with their church not realising that they are actually FAMILY . . . designed to do life together."[20]

The truth is, we who are believers all share the responsibility to gather ourselves in the local church, and then plant ourselves there, so that we can flourish. That's what the Bible says. If you want to thrive throughout life, make sure you have roots in the house of God.[21] Don't just visit, stay. Drop your anchor. You will find support, instruction, comfort, and companionship as you navigate the storm.

We are to dwell in the house of God, as the psalmist says. What does "dwell" mean? Well, it means we do life in the house of God. If we are part of God's family, we don't just show up for services and then run out the door, any more than doing life with our immediate family means we just show up at mealtimes. Over the years at the Wagner house, members of my family have definitely popped in when dinner is on the table, but they have also contributed to the running of our home. We all have chores to make home a great place to be. (Some members are quicker to do their chores than others.) We spend time together. We talk. My husband and I have helped with homework. We have shared doing the dishes and the vacuuming. We hug . . . laugh . . . cry . . . sing . . . work . . . ask for help . . . admit mistakes. All of this happens in our home; I think it should happen in the house of God too.

Pick an area of church life and help. If you can sing in key through an entire song (never happens for me), think about joining the worship team. If you can smile, how about being a greeter at the door? If you love children—at least most of the time!—help in the children's ministry. How about computers—can you work them? Maybe the office could use a volunteer. How about joining the outreach team as they clean the neighborhood or visit the elderly? Or could you finance a young person to go to camp? Find an area of service and give. It's all part of dwelling in God's house.

Be present when the doors are open. Don't just tolerate the church service. Smile at people. Hey, maybe the pastor will say something great today, so be ready to take notes! Ya know, really take notes—don't just look at your Instagram feed! Don't make church a place where you spend an hour on Sunday. Make it a place where you dwell. It should be a place where real people with real lives and real problems can get real help as they worship a real God.

Remember the story I told you about the depressed girl who went to the club and ultimately ended up having sex with a stranger? While she definitely had struggles to overcome, she dropped this anchor. She came into the house of God and started to engage with people. She joined a

small group of women who loved on her, and she got help as she dealt
with the health issues involved. She was front and center during worship,
often crying, as the Spirit of God brought healing. She took notes during
messages. She made church a place to dwell. Eventually she became the
one helping other young girls overcome their challenges.

Philip and I have received so many letters over the years from people
who came to Oasis Church in the midst of a storm. The letters were ad-
dressed to Philip and me specifically, but it is the family of God they
connected with in church that helped them make it safely to shore.

Dear Philip and Holly,

I was invited to your church by a friend and decided to come.
I guess she could see that my life was in chaos! I was convinced
that divorce from my husband was the only option. Our marriage
truly was a disaster. But we came to the church, broken hearts
and all, and began to learn how to be champions. We have made
friends we will have for years to come. We learned how to build
a healthy marriage. Thank you for what you give of yourselves
every day. . . . Thank you for making this church a place where
hurting people can come in and get help.

Dear Philip and Holly,

I came to the church a total mess—although I wasn't willing
to admit that I was. I have been dealing with issues in my heart
that came from being sexually abused as a child. Because of all of
this, many aspects of my life were not great. When I walked into
the church for the first time, I felt like I was home . . . to one of
the first I had ever experienced. It took me a while to understand
the unconditional love of God, but I did feel loved and cared for.
I began a relationship with Jesus that was more than religion . . .
it has changed my life. I met people who truly seemed to care. I
was then free to work on the issues of my heart. Thank you for

loving, thank you for demonstrating His love to me. I am so
grateful for this church and the people I now call family.

In the midst of your storm, make sure you drop anchor in the house
of God. You will grow, make friends who can help you reach shore, and
encounter the God who calms troubled seas.

It's time to drop your anchors. Let's not forget that the goal of Paul's
trip in Acts 27 was ultimately to get to Rome. Your life has a goal too. I
don't know what it is, but you do. Those sailors forgot where they were
headed when they were in the midst of the raging storm. They took their
eyes off the target and focused on the waves. If Paul hadn't been on board
making good decisions, all might have been lost.

The waves may keep coming, but don't let them distract you. As Paul
instructed, find your brave by dropping your four anchors. They will
steady you in the midst of the turmoil.

So how ya doing? Does dropping anchors seem impossible, especially
as wave after wave is crashing against you? Why not take a moment right
now, breathe in deeply, and pray, asking God to help you drop your anchors? You will get through this. You are not alone. Find your brave, my
friend and my fellow storm traveler. Start by dropping two anchors today:
remember who you are and why you are here. Don't let the Enemy con-
fuse you. You're too precious in God's eyes for that.

Don't Quit!

God is within her, she will not fall;
God will help her at break of day.

—Psalm 46:5

In times of difficulty, you may feel that
your problems will go on and on. But
they won't. Every mountain has a top.
Every problem has a life span. The
question is, who is going to give in first,
the frustration or you?

—Dr. Robert H. Schuller

You are going to want to give up. Don't.

—Unknown

When my son was seven, I joined him in taking karate. One of the reasons I did was because I needed a task that I could start and finish. Getting from white belt to black belt was the challenge I set before myself. Might have been easier to learn to knit a sweater and finish that. Oh right, I forgot, I did start a sweater and didn't finish it. So on to karate. I showed up on day one with my new white uniform and stiff new

white belt. I had seen the brochures; I knew this was going to be exciting. I had also seen the movie *The Karate Kid*—the way-better-original
one—and I wanted to learn to do the amazing kick from the end of the
movie. Remember that one? (If you were born after 1985, just shut up.) I
knew it wouldn't be long before I wowed my family and friends with my
incredible ability.

Well, we didn't learn that amazing kick the first day. Or even the
fortieth day. For months, we learned how to fall. Really? This is what I
paid eighty-five dollars a month for? I spent hours learning how to fall to
the front, how to fall on my back, how to fall to the side. Fall. Get up. Fall.
Get up. Fall. Get up.

Boring!

I wanted to quit.

But that had been my pattern for years. As soon as a project got a
little mundane or slightly boring, I would quit, feeling justified, because
why should I have to put up with boring? And then I would look for
something more exciting.

But this time I didn't quit, because I kept looking at that black belt
on the wall in hopes of it one day being mine.

A few years into the karate challenge, it became inconvenient trying
to balance work, family, and my karate life. I almost quit at that point.

Three years into my study of karate, it finally dawned on me that this
was a contact sport. We were sparring by this point, and I ended up with
more bruises and broken toes than I had bargained for. Maybe my goal
had been too ambitious. What had I been thinking anyway?

Four and a half years later, I passed my black-belt test. I am now officially dangerous. I had started something. And I finished it. Yay me!
The black-belt test was one of the hardest physical challenges I have ever
undergone. For the first three hours I demonstrated all the moves and
forms (intricate fighting moves). Even though I was absolutely exhausted,
the panel of black belts testing me kept giving me more and more to do.

I felt like I was about to drop, which is when my teacher said, "Holly, put on your gear. It is now time to fight." *What?* I had nothing left in me with which to fight. My arms and legs were shaking. My brain was dead. I felt like I was going to throw up. I kept thinking, *I am definitely going to get beat up.* (Of course I said none of this out loud—I didn't want them to think I was a complete loser.)

I put on my gear and moved to the center of the mat to fight a second-degree black belt. I didn't have to win. I just had to fight him. Good thing, because by this time I was simply trying to stay upright. He threw the first punch, and I blocked it. He threw another one, and I blocked that one. My muscles were moving before my brain could even engage. He did get a few punches in (okay, a lot), and I ended up on the ground several times, but my muscle memory kicked in many times. And when I received my black belt, I was so grateful that I'd stayed the course and didn't give in when all I really wanted to do was quit!

I have heard some athletes claim that exhaustion can improve their performance by shifting them from reason to instinct. They achieve things in their instinctive output of energy they would not be able to do if they were figuring out things mentally. The training kicks in and takes them to the finish. Those athletes have a lot to teach us about persevering in the midst of our storms. What we have deliberately woven into our lives—the way we think, our habits—can carry us to the shore. All of the things we have talked about in the earlier chapters—choosing our thoughts, being mindful of the people we surround ourselves with, getting rid of baggage, dropping anchors—help us stay the course. Forgive me for being cheesy, but those things will be the wind in our sails when we're tempted to quit.

Wanting to quit in the midst of the storm is understandable. You just want to make the challenge or the pain go away. I get it. Sometimes as the waves crash against us, we get tired. And weariness causes us to want to give up. Quit moving forward. Quit walking out our purpose. Many times this last year, as wave after wave hit my life, I asked myself if this (fulfilling purpose, staying on course) was worth it. Because in the middle of the waves, it is hard to believe that God can bring anything good out of it, and does it *really* matter if I quit?

It matters.

This is the moment to find your brave. To keep going. One definition of *quit* is simply to give up, to admit defeat. Now, I may look defeated, I may feel defeated, but I am not going to admit defeat. Wanting to quit isn't bad. It is the actual quitting that will keep us from the shore we were destined to reach. Can we keep going? Can we finish what we have started?

STAY IN THE BOAT

The sailors on Paul's ship wanted to quit. They were tired of the battery of waves. They were weary of the dark nights. They were afraid, and they doubted they would make it. They had been told to drop anchors, which they did from the back of the ship. Then, some of the sailors headed to the front of the ship, and while pretending to drop more anchors, they tried to sneak off the ship by slipping away in the lifeboat. Paul saw what they were doing and went to the commanding officer with some words of advice.

> Unless these men stay with the ship,
> you cannot be saved.
> —Acts 27:31

Paul told the guards on the ship, "You will all die unless the sailors stay aboard." Basically he was telling them, "Don't quit." In the middle of a storm, when the ship is at risk, the skill of every sailor is needed, and yet these sailors were trying to save themselves; they didn't even consider anyone else on the boat. Paul had told them previously that they all would be saved, but now they doubted and just wanted out. I am not sure why those sailors thought a smaller boat would be safer, but often in the midst of a storm we do not think clearly—we just want to get away. We are not thinking of consequences to us or anyone else, we are just tired of the storm. But as Paul shows us, our decision to quit, to jump ship, affects not only us but also those around us.

If you leave a marriage in the middle of a storm, your children and grandchildren will be affected. What will be the consequences if you leave your job? You might feel free, but what about others? Did you just give them more to do? Timing is everything.

How about your church? Every church goes through storms. Don't bail out during one. It might affect younger believers who need to see faithfulness. Are you in the middle of a project that God has trusted you with? Has it gotten hard and you just want to quit? Who would be affected if you did? Let's be those women who can be trusted to stay the course in the midst of a storm and not opt to bail out.

What Women Can Do—When They Don't Quit in the Storm

One dictionary definition of *quitting* is "to abandon necessary action." Just as athletes keep training through the pain for a chance at a medal, you and I must not abandon certain actions if we are going to arrive victorious on the shore.

Fortunately, we have great role models to show us how to persevere through rough storms. Where would we be if some of the amazing people in history had quit their journeys simply because the challenges were too much?

Susan B. Anthony was ridiculed and persecuted simply because she thought every human being ought to be treated with dignity. She encountered armed threats and cruel crowds. In 1856, the townspeople of Syracuse, New York, hanged her in effigy, then dragged her image through the streets. Still, in 1863, Susan helped organize a Women's Loyal National League to support and petition for the Thirteenth Amendment, which would outlaw slavery, and two years later it passed.

She then campaigned for the rights of African Americans and for women's full citizenship, including the right to vote, in the Fourteenth and Fifteenth Amendments. I am sure she was disappointed when the rights guaranteed by those amendments did not extend to women, but she didn't give up. A storm was raging all around her, but she didn't abandon ship. She persevered in spite of huge obstacles. I am sure at times she grew weary, but I am also sure she knew that the goal was always more important than her momentary discomfort.

Susan died in 1906. It wasn't until 1920 that women achieved the right to vote in the United States.[1] She didn't get to see that dream realized. But still, she persevered for you and for me. Can you keep going, knowing that not only will there be others who would be hurt by your quitting but also others who will benefit from your determination not to quit? Can you see past the frustration and pain of this moment and keep going?

Another heroine was only five when an illness left her partially blind, and then her mother died a few years later. After her father abandoned her, she lived in an orphanage. Obviously this young girl faced huge obstacles—her storm probably seemed unconquerable. But she didn't let the storms keep her down for long. After she underwent surgery that restored some of her sight, she had an unsuccessful trial run as a housekeeper. It was then she realized that getting an education was her best hope. A man visiting the orphanage heard of her insatiable passion for education and her desire to go to school, so he arranged for her to go to

Perkins Institution for the Blind in Boston. In spite of the difficulties, she loved it and gradually learned to read using Braille.

She eventually graduated first in her class. In 1887, she moved to Alabama to become the teacher and caretaker of a deaf-blind child. The child was Helen Keller, and the woman who persevered through all of the difficulties was Anne Sullivan. Through Anne's creativity, discipline, persistence, and patience, she was able to reach and then ultimately teach Helen. Thanks to Anne's brave perseverance, and against all odds, her student, Helen, eventually attended Radcliffe College and graduated with honors.

As Helen's teacher, Anne pioneered techniques of education for the disabled and lobbied for increased opportunities for those without sight. Because of Anne's teaching success, Helen's life became an inspiration for many.[2]

If these women had quit and jumped ship, history would look very different. They were just ordinary women—who refused to give in. Even when it got hard. Even when they didn't see the result they wanted.

What has God entrusted you with? No matter what it is, it won't come without a storm or two or ten. Are you in college? Don't quit even though you might have five assignments due and your lab partner isn't carrying her share. Don't quit giving your all when you are passed over for a promotion and wonder if anyone recognizes your abilities. If you have started to get healthy, don't quit. Even though every muscle aches, and you really want just that one little scoop of ice cream, and your fitness partner has gone back to eating junk. Don't quit that commitment to purity even though all around you hear how old-fashioned and out of touch you are. Don't quit that marriage even though you want to. Don't quit pursuing God even though your prayers for a loved one battling cancer were answered with a funeral rather than a miracle and now you question your faith. Don't resign yourself. Don't let the whispers of the Enemy cause you to lose your confidence. Don't lose your joy. Who knows all that waits on the other side of your determination not to quit?

A college degree? A healthy body? A strong family? A more determined faith?

One thing is certain: if you quit, you never will know what could have been.

Not Quitting Takes Determination

The biblical book of Ruth details a great story. We learn that a woman named Naomi is married to Elimelech, and they have two sons. They are Israelites living in Moab, a land filled with people who do not know the God of Israel. Both of their sons marry Moabite women: Ruth and Orpah. At some point, all the men in the family die. Naomi decides she wants to return to the land of her forefathers, so she chooses to go back to Bethlehem, her hometown. At that time, to be a childless widow was to be a member of one the lowest and most disadvantaged classes. Widows lived almost entirely on the support of others. Since Naomi has no family in Moab, and no one else to help her, she is desperate.

As she prepares to leave, she asks her daughters-in-law to stay in Moab, where at least life is familiar, and yet both say, "No, we are coming with you." They begin the thirty-mile trip together. Not only are they all grieving, but they have to deal with the dangerous journey. They are vulnerable widows taking a trip few women would dare to take without a man. There are no paved roads, and they are easy prey for bandits. They are also faced with the challenge of crossing the Jordan River and climbing a two-thousand-foot hill.[3] At one point, Naomi again asks the young women to return to Moab and Orpah agrees; the journey ahead just looks too hard. (The unknown always does.) But Ruth refuses to go back, and the Bible tells us that when Naomi sees that Ruth is determined to go with her, she says nothing more.[4]

Not quitting takes determination, and determination can be seen. Determination is not just something that is felt—it is evident to others around you.

I think determination is what is missing in so many situations today. The determination to follow through.

The determination to seek God until we find Him.

The determination to keep building that marriage.

The determination to keep applying for jobs.

The determination to live a healthy lifestyle.

I have found that God never asks us to do something hard. He always asks us to do something impossible!

C'mon, think about it—one-hundred-year-old Sarah having a baby is not hard . . . it is impossible! But with God, it became possible.

Parting the Red Sea with a staff was not hard . . . it was impossible. But with God, it became possible.

Providing a crowd of more than five thousand people with food using only a few fish and loaves was not hard . . . it was impossible. But with God, it became possible.

It might seem impossible to pick up the pieces after a broken relationship, but with God, it is possible.

Finishing that degree when you've got a job and a family might seem impossible, but with God, it is possible.

Determination to keep going and to trust God is what makes it happen, and determination requires perseverance. The apostle James explains it like this: "Consider it pure joy, my brothers and sisters, whenever you face trials of many kinds, because you know that the testing of your faith produces perseverance. Let perseverance finish its work so that you may be mature and complete, not lacking anything."[5]

That's the ultimate goal, isn't it? To become *mature* and *complete*. Maturity does not come from how much we know but through how much we persevere. God is all about the journey. What He is doing in you is as important as what He will do through you. Don't quit while the process is still happening!

Perseverance is the key, and I have found it applies only to the difficult. I have never had to persevere through a massage. Or a manicure. Or a triple-shot macchiato. It is only in navigating the challenges and the trials that we are made complete.

The disciples learned to find their brave as they traversed a stormy sea. One of my favorite Bible stories takes place right after Jesus and the disciples fed five-thousand-plus people with a couple of tuna sandwiches. Remember that? A young boy had surrendered his lunch to Jesus, and Jesus did what only He could do and multiplied it so that it fed the large crowd. I would imagine the disciples were beside themselves! This was quite the miracle. How fun is ministry! Right after this happened, Jesus immediately made His disciples get in a boat and go ahead of Him, telling them that He would meet them on the other side of the lake.[6]

The disciples were in the boat, rowing toward the other side. At first I imagine they were all excitedly talking about the miracle they had just witnessed. Maybe, just because they were boys, they were competing a bit. (Okay, maybe we girls do that too.)

"I had more fish in my basket than you did."

"*I* always knew Jesus was going to do that!"

Just some friendly competition and goofing off. But then the Bible says that when they were in the middle of the sea, the wind became stronger and they struggled with the oars.[7] As the wind-driven waves crashed against their boat, they probably started thinking, *What are we doing here? This is hard. Feeding people was fun and easy. Let's go back there!* They didn't know that, ultimately, if they pressed through to the other shore, they would end up in Gennesaret, where there were people who needed miracles.

We don't always know what is ahead, and we never will if we don't persevere through what is in our now. I am sure the disciples were getting tired; I am sure they were afraid. The wind and waves were crashing against their boat, and perhaps they were in real danger.

Jesus, who doesn't always use a boat (remember?), started walking on the water. He was going where He said He would meet them. The other side. The Bible tells us that Jesus saw His disciples straining at the oars, yet "He was about to pass by them."[8] What?

He was just going to walk right past them?

Why?

I don't know. Maybe because He had told them to go to the other side and He knew they had the ability to do that. If we read the rest of Mark 6, we find out that when the disciples saw Jesus, they cried out. Well, actually, at first they didn't know who He was. Really? How many people do they know who walk on water? But once they realized that it was Jesus, they called His name, and He calmed the wind and waves and then got in their boat.

Like the disciples, I had to find my brave in the middle of a storm. Ten years ago I was rowing my little boat, when suddenly I was diagnosed with breast cancer. I thought, *Hey, I liked it better back there—before the hundreds of doctor visits, before the pain, before the surgery, before the treatments.* I had a similar thought before all the storms hit my life last year—and yet the journey with God is always ahead. Every time I want to return to the past, by reminiscing about what used to be or holding on to sentimental attachments, I remember that He has given me all I need to get to the other side of the shore. Many times when I have called on His name, He has gotten in my boat, calming the wind and waves raging in my soul. He will get in your boat too. Finding your brave in the midst of the storm takes determination. Please. Don't. Quit.

When the apostle Paul was in prison awaiting execution, he wrote some powerful words to his protégé, Timothy. In his final letter, he offered wisdom about the church, life, and the future. And he cast one last look over his shoulder, summarizing his own life: "I have fought the good fight, I have finished the race, I have kept the faith."[9]

Paul was a great man! Whole cities came to know God because of him, and he introduced the continent of Europe to the gospel. His secret to greatness wasn't in his knowledge, though—and he was a knowledgeable guy. It wasn't in his looks. It wasn't because of his eloquence. It wasn't even in his talents. Paul was extraordinary because he did not quit—no matter what circumstances befell him.

After his conversion experience, Paul found the people around him hostile; they despised and mocked him. He could have said, "There is no love here. I'm throwing in the towel." But he didn't. Then the Christians didn't believe his conversion, and the Jews tried to kill him. He didn't give up. Paul was thrown into prison more than once. He didn't quit.

When he said yes to Jesus, he was all in. Before his conversion, he had persecuted and killed Christians. Like all of us he had been forgiven much. He knew what his calling was: to take the gospel to the Gentiles, and no matter what got in the way, he persevered through it. He kept his eyes on Jesus. He did not quit.

He endured a cruel crowd's stoning him and leaving him for dead. How did he respond? He got up and returned to the city filled with the very people who wanted to kill him.[10] Even in the midst of the literal storm and shipwreck that we're focusing on in this book, he still didn't quit. Paul instructed the sailors to stay with the ship. Yes, the storm was raging, and yes, they wanted to leave. But their idea of escaping using the small lifeboat was not a good plan anyway. Most escape plans aren't.

Paul had plenty of opportunities to quit—to claim that his life was just too hard. But he didn't.

There will be plenty of opportunities for us to quit too. We can't take them—no matter how hard the journey is, no matter how high the waves are! Make the decision to be all in. You have been entrusted with a calling. Don't abandon it.

You Are Surrounded

Please know that as you go through your storm, you are surrounded by all the heroes of our faith who have gone before us. The writer of Hebrews puts it this way:

All these pioneers who blazed the way, all these veterans cheering
us on? It means we'd better get on with it. Strip down, start
running—and never quit! No extra spiritual fat, no parasitic
sins. Keep your eyes on *Jesus,* who both began and finished this
race we're in. Study how he did it. Because he never lost sight
of where he was headed—that exhilarating finish in and with
God—he could put up with anything along the way.[11]

Know that as you find your brave, all the hosts of heaven are cheering
you on. You must make it through. You cannot let this storm sink you. A
whole generation of people needs you to hand them the baton. They need
the wisdom you will gain from getting through this storm. Maybe it is
actually selfish of us to give up in tough times. Or do you think that is too
strong a word? I just think there are people we are supposed to help—
right on the other side of this storm. That is why we can't quit. It is not
just about us. That's part of the maturity James talked about. That's what
Paul understood. You count. Finding your brave counts.

Gideon was a man chosen by God to be a leader and judge of Israel
during one of the nation's dark times. Gideon, full of fear and insecurity,
doubted his ability to lead the people, but an angel of God assured him
of God's presence. At one point Gideon and his small army of three hundred were to defeat the Midianites, their enemies. As they were in battle,
the Bible describes them as "exhausted yet keeping up the pursuit."[12] The
enemy was defeated and scattered. In order to capture them, even though
at this point they were hungry and tired, Gideon's army had no choice
but to continue the pursuit. They could see that victory was possible.
They were willing to take the battle to the gates—to finish it.

Philip and I spent some time a few years ago in Jerusalem. A wall surrounds the old city of Jerusalem and features seven gates into the city. We
walked in and out of a few of them. I learned that in any Israelite city,
which was encircled by huge walls, it was a battle at the gates that many
times decided who won a war and which culture would influence the land.

Similar to Paul choosing to persevere to the shore—and encouraging others to do so too—Gideon took his battle all the way to the gate. Can you? Can you get through whatever battle you are fighting, whatever storm is trying to take you out? The prophet Isaiah encourages us by saying that God is a source of strength "to those who turn back the battle at the gate."[13] When you are at your weakest, He shows up.

So stay the course. Keep persevering through the storm. The benefits of not quitting are huge.

You will be stronger.

You will reach your shore.

The people in your world will be encouraged—and possibly changed for the better.

Find your brave and determine not to quit. Keep believing in the One who can calm the storm.

Stronger

You never know how strong you are until being
strong is the only choice you have.

—Bob Marley

To every man there comes in his lifetime that
special moment when he is figuratively tapped
on the shoulder and offered a chance to do a
very special thing, unique to him and fitted
to his talents. What a tragedy if that moment
finds him unprepared or unqualified for the
work which would be his finest hour.

—Winston Churchill

knew a woman who was on a serious diet. She had to lose more than one
hundred pounds—no easy feat. She was doing well, when suddenly
some work stuff came up that stressed her out. People in her office were
being moved into different positions, and no one was sure he or she would
have a job the next day. Her job description changed regularly. It's understandable that she felt tossed about. She started to think, *There's too much
going on right now. I'm too upset. I think I'll have that pizza.* She gave

up her diet, gained back the previously lost pounds (plus some more), and felt more discouraged than ever.

Another woman faced a storm in her marriage. She and her husband seemed to be drifting apart, and she was scared. He was working more and more hours, and they couldn't find time to connect. She just about stopped eating. Her energy level dropped, her temper sharpened, and she was even less able to give to the marriage.

Another woman had just lost her mother. She and her mom hadn't been close, but now they wouldn't ever get that opportunity. Her sadness affected every area of her life; soon all she could do was sit on the sofa in the dark. She didn't shower or eat. She lapsed beyond grief and into depression.

All of these storms are serious, and I am aware that they are painful. In the middle of our storms, especially as past hurts surface, the challenges often make us feel like pulling the sheet over our head and never getting out of bed again. From my own experience and from hearing other people's stories, I can tell you that if we are going to make it through the storms, we *must* build our strength. The Bible tells us that if we "falter in a time of trouble, how small is [our] strength!"[1] Life is full of adversity, so we need to make sure we have the strength to pull through. Let's get our strength-training routine figured out.

LIVE STRONG

The sailors were tired. They had been battling this storm for days. They hadn't had much to eat and certainly hadn't gotten much rest. And probably the last thing they wanted to do when they were seasick was eat! But Paul knew that's exactly what they needed to do. If they lost their strength, they'd be worse off. So he encouraged them to take a moment and refuel their bodies. Big challenges lay ahead, including a swim in the sea toward shore, so they needed to feed their bodies the fuel to make it.

That's an important reminder for us. When trouble comes, we need to give our bodies the essentials so they can do their jobs. Notice I said *essentials.*

One of the practical things we can do in everyday life and certainly in the midst of challenges is to develop strength. We will need real strength as we navigate the adversity we will face and the challenges ahead of us. Practical, real strength.

After my cancer diagnosis, I started taking Proverbs 31:17 personally: "She girds herself with strength [spiritual, mental, and physical fitness for her God-given task] and makes her arms strong and firm."[2]

I urge you to eat something now.
You'll need strength for the rescue ahead.

—Acts 27:34, MSG

There is a strength that comes from our God. He is our strength, and yet the strength that this verse talks about is strength that *we* ourselves can build. "She girds *herself.*" This strength, which is necessary in order to get through storms, does not descend from a cloud or come from a magic pill (sometimes I am sad about this). This strength grows in us as we do a few specific things. If we are going to do whatever it is that God has asked of us, and get through whatever difficult situation we need to, then we must have those three types of strength: physical, mental, and spiritual. And strength is built by pushing through resistance—allowing that wind to bend us but not break us. Or to put it another way: think biceps. I am sure yours are amazing, and they did not get that way by watching someone else lift weights. So it's time to get off the spectator's bench and start building strength.

Let's start with where Paul started and get something to eat.

LET'S GET PHYSICAL

Some of us don't eat, as Paul's shipmates didn't, when storms hit, and we need to. Others of us, ahem, eat the wrong things. Personally, I can't imagine being so stressed that I can't eat. And when I am stressed, I want carbs! Not salad and grilled veggies. I want french fries. Bread. Ice cream. Chocolate. Pizza. I am now making myself hungry! Even during times of turmoil, somehow I always find time to put food in my mouth!

We need to eat and keep our bodies strong and healthy—and that means giving it the *right* things. In the midst of my cancer storm, I decided that I wanted to get healthy. Nothing like a cancer diagnosis to wake you up to health! If I was going to reach my shore, I needed to strengthen my body. I read dozens of books about health, and I made changes so that I could be fit. I changed what I ate, when I slept, and how I exercised. I knew that in order for me to get healthy, it was going to take more than eating one salad. I had to make drastic health changes. One change I made was to throw out everything in my pantry that didn't build strength in my body, such as white sugar, white flour, and most things with preservatives. (That was a fun day in my marriage. Not.) I had to switch gears mentally and then switch them physically. That meant

- shopping at new stores, where they sell very strange natural products
- cooking organic foods
- learning about juicing veggies
- drinking wheatgrass
- swallowing forty-plus vitamins a day
- reading stacks of health books
- exercising regularly

For years I think I was just unconscious to the fact that I have an obligation to be as healthy as possible. Our bodies are the temples of the Holy Spirit. We are supposed to honor Him with our bodies, which means we can't treat them carelessly.[3] I realized others were counting on me to get through this storm—not just my family and friends, but others who need to know about Jesus and His power at work within us. I needed to take care of the only body I have been given so that I could finish strong.

For years I abused my body (I ate whatever I wanted, I stopped exercising, and I did not get enough sleep), thinking that it would just bounce back. And for years it did. I would hear about healthy eating and the importance of exercising from time to time, but I never really applied what I learned.

It just seemed too hard.

And expensive.

And certainly not convenient.

Well.

Getting cancer was harder.

More expensive.

And definitely more inconvenient.

So finally I found my brave, as I was willing to learn what it takes to get and stay healthy.

I am now going to get into your business a little. Okay, a lot. Let me ask, are you taking care of the one and only body you have been given? Are you strengthening it? You and I have been given one body to see us through all the seasons and storms of life. We need to care for our bodies and do our best to keep them strong.

As I went through the cancer battle, I realized that I have a responsibility to do my part in staying healthy, in building strength in my body. When I read what Paul wrote to the Corinthians, I felt challenged enough to change:

> Do you not know that in a race all the runners compete, but
> [only] one receives the prize? So run [your race] that you may
> lay hold [of the prize] and make it yours.

Now every athlete who goes into training conducts himself temperately and restricts himself in all things. They do it to win a wreath that will soon wither, but we [do it to receive a crown of eternal blessedness] that cannot wither.

Therefore I do not run uncertainly (without definite aim). I do not box like one beating the air and striking without an adversary.

But [like a boxer] I buffet my body [handle it roughly, discipline it by hardships] and subdue it, for fear that after proclaiming to others the Gospel and things pertaining to it, I myself should become unfit [not stand the test, be unapproved and rejected as a counterfeit].[4]

Paul was comparing himself to the runners and contestants in the Isthmian Games, well known by the Corinthians. Those competing in the games were on strict diets and exercised rigorously. The athletes disciplined the desires of their bodies, and they did it all to obtain a prize that would perish—basically a crown of leaves that only one winner could claim. But Christianity is not a race in which there is only one winner. Paul encouraged each of us to run to win—we can all win. You and I are living and running our race, not to get an award that will perish but to hear Jesus say, "Well done." So shouldn't we *even more* exercise self-control? Rather than our bodies telling our minds what to do, shouldn't our minds tell our bodies what to eat, how to rest, when to exercise? We all want to finish our race strong, and that will take intention. Regardless of what storm you are in or might be in in the future, you will need strength to get through it.

I finally realized this when I was diagnosed with cancer. I started regularly exercising. But just so ya know, I never *feel* like exercising. I know some people just love it. Well, God bless those people, but I don't love it. I just do it because I am committed to building strength. I don't spend hours in the gym—just about forty-five minutes. And actually I found a great place online, DailyBurn.com, that allows me to choose different forms of exercise that I can do from anywhere, at home or even at a hotel when I travel.

I changed my sleeping patterns. I learned that our immune system reboots in the middle of the night when we are sleeping, so to the best of my ability, I try to be in bed by 11:00 p.m. Sometimes life and all its craziness gets in the way, but that is my goal. Since I have learned what true health is, I'm making every effort to take care of the body that God has entrusted me with. Dr. Myron Wentz, one of the doctors who helped me get stronger, put it like this:

> True health is not simply how you feel when you wake up each morning. Nor is it a favorable lab, radiology, or physical exam report from your physician. True health is not based on the sculpture of your physique nor your ability to compete in a triathlon.
>
> True health is being absolutely the best you can be with the conditions you were given and the situation in which you now live. True health is not just the absence of disease. It is empowering our bodies to perform at their optimum level.
>
> When I think of optimal health, I think of energy and stamina. I think of flexibility, strength, and endurance. Optimal health means having reserves to deal with the unexpected stresses encountered in everyday life. . . .
>
> Good health cannot and must not be taken for granted. It should be guarded, with utmost security and attention, every day of your life. That is the most effective way to avoid degenerative disease and thus to achieve the maximum number of years of active, enjoyable living. Only by maintaining good health can you do what you want to do and need to do for yourself and your loved ones.[5]

I learned that fewer Americans are dying of contagious diseases and more are dying from degenerative ones. I learned that the fuel we put into our bodies and how we deal with our toxic environment matter. I finally heard what the US Surgeon General said more than twenty years ago: "What we eat may affect our risk for several of the leading causes of death for Americans, notably, coronary heart disease, stroke, atherosclerosis, diabetes, and some types of cancer. These disorders together now account for more than two-thirds of all deaths in the United States."[6]

How ya doing so far? Still with me? Ready to find your brave and begin the physical strength-building process?

I know this can seem overwhelming. I spent a few weeks at a holistic hospital, learning about stress and environmental toxins. One woman, a patient who'd had a double mastectomy and recently learned that the cancer was now in her lungs, said that she was moving to West Virginia where the air was clear. She was going to live in a small community and play her ukulele. No kidding. I thought, *Maybe I should move to West Virginia and play the ukulele too. That would be a lot less stressful than LA!*

I went back to my room wondering how I was going to tell Philip that we were moving. My friend Bobbie was visiting with me, and as I walked into the room, she could tell something was wrong. When I told her that I needed to move to West Virginia where the air was clean and there would be less stress, she laughed. She grabbed my face, looked into my eyes, and reminded me that the same God who called me to LA would take care of me in LA. She basically told me to snap out of it. Destiny has a geography! But once again, I had been tempted to leave the place where God had called me to live and work. I am fairly sure Philip would not have gone for the whole West Virginia thing (no professional sports teams).

Another reason we need our strength during a storm is that we can get weary, then depressed. And while some of weathering the storm has to do with gaining mental strength, it also has a physical root. I know plenty of people on antidepressants that have made a big difference to their overall well-being. I also know that the pills are not the whole answer. There are some practical, physical things we must do.

Physical activity is crucial if we are going to stay healthy for a lifetime, and it is important that we don't neglect it during a storm. Researchers at Duke, Harvard, and Stanford universities have shown repeatedly that exercise is powerful medicine for both anxiety (which is what we generally feel during a storm!) and depression (another common side effect). The Duke team found that adults with major depression who worked out every day (a half hour of aerobics, fifteen minutes each of warm-up and cool down) did just as well after four months as a group taking Zoloft. In a six-month follow-up, the exercisers were more likely to be partially or fully recovered than those on medication, and less likely to relapse—8 percent versus 38 percent.[7]

I am not telling you to go off any medications. I am simply suggesting that in the midst of the hard times you should work to keep your body strong. Regular exercise will go a long way toward seeing you to shore.

I work out, not because I am trying to win a bodybuilding contest (that will never happen), but because I am trying to build muscles, keep my heart healthy, and limit my percentage of body fat to a reasonable level. I have scoliosis and can often experience pain in my back. I have found, however, that if I strengthen my abdominal muscles, my back is stronger and hurts less. Do you know how I strengthen my abs? By doing hundreds of different kinds of stomach crunches, leg lifts, and sit-ups. Is doing them ever fun? No! But I do them anyway, because I know I need to be strong to accomplish all that I have been put here to do and to more effectively fight off the Enemy's lies that come hard and fast during a storm.

Also, by taking care of my physical body, I have found that I just feel better. And when I feel good, I make better decisions than when I am physically weak. When I am physically weak, the storms seem so huge and the shore so far away and then the little things completely overwhelm me. We have big lives to live and some serious storms to endure, so let's get strong! I don't care if you are eighteen or seventy-eight, you can start now to do something physically that will help you weather the storm.

Another part of remaining physically strong is remembering to rest. Did you know that muscle actually grows in the rest periods? We work a muscle, rest it, and work it again. We need rest for our bodies to recover. In the midst of a crisis, it is easy to work so hard that we forget to rest. But if we are going to reach the shore, we must rest! God worked hard for six days, then He rested. He wants us to do the same (that's why the Sabbath is one of the Ten Commandments).

During my cancer storm, I knew someone else who was going through a storm at work. She did get days off, but on those days, she did not do things that replenished her soul. So when she went back to work, she was just as worn out as when she left. Rest should involve replenishing not only the body but also the soul.

What is restful for you? Find out what that is. It might include reading, going for a walk, having coffee with a friend, sleeping, praying, worshiping, watching a movie, enjoying a dinner out . . . whatever. Just make sure you take moments of rest—physically, emotionally, mentally, and spiritually—in the midst of your storm.

As we have been talking about, life is not without stress. Daily we will face intense situations, and they won't all go away. So how we handle the stress is really what is important. During my two-week hospital stay for cancer treatment, one of the doctors performed a test that measured my stress level. Before the test began, he asked me how stressed I was feeling. I told them that I honestly felt fine. He hooked me up to a machine and did the test.

The results shocked me. He said that my stress level was as if I were staring a roaring lion in the face.

A roaring lion.

In the face.

And the shocking thing was, I couldn't tell. (Obviously I needed to get better at recognizing and handling stress!)

So how ya doing? Let me remind you that growing strength in any area takes time. This can be frustrating because we live in a microwave society. Everything is practically instant: fast food, Amazon deliveries, e-mails, cell phones, travel—even our pharmacies and Starbucks are drive-through! We want it when we want it, and we want it right *now*! But building real strength takes time. So take a breath. Then take one step today toward building physical strength. Listen to Paul: eat something healthy, get moving, and then rest.

BUILDING MENTAL STRENGTH

Physical strength is just one part of the strength we are to build, mental strength is another. So now it's time to put our minds to work. Remember that word *chayil* from Proverbs 31? It means that we are a force on the earth. *Chayil* actually consists of power through three things: people, means, and resources. The Proverbs 31 woman is a force on the earth because she knows how to build relationships with people. She is a force on the earth because she knows how to make money and wisely spend it (got that second part down?). And she is a force on the earth because she resources her life. She is a learner: She reads books and stretches her mind. She is gaining mental strength. And she's a model for us.

Let's be those women who do more than watch reality TV; let's be those women who are not only learning more information and more skills but also learning new ways of thinking about the world, problem solving, life, and people.

Several years ago I decided to go back to school to earn my masters in theology. I might be 103 when I finally get it, but I have started and am reading very thick textbooks. I have to write papers that explain the doctrine of God, the hypostatic union (what?), and what a biblical worldview

looks like. I am not sure where furthering my education will end; I just
wanted to begin. And I've already discovered that increasing my mental
strength has broadened my thinking, which in turn has allowed me to
get creative and think bigger in the midst of storms.

Maybe school is not your thing. No problem. Find another way to
increase your mental strength. Maybe read a book by someone you don't
agree with, or get to know a person from a different culture. You could
visit another country or attend a writing, business, or art program. The
list is endless.

Mental strength doesn't stop there, though. It consists of another
layer: our emotions and how well we handle them in the midst of our
challenges.

Do you control your emotions, or do they lead you? Can you control
your anger? Your words? Is courage being enlarged in you? Or is fear taking root?

Do you struggle with jealousy, or can you rest in the security of who
God says you are? Do you choose

- love or hate?
- peace or chaos?
- joy or sorrow?
- humility or pride?

One of our greatest challenges during a difficult season is to manage
our emotions. That's all part of self-control, which is part of mental
strength. In the midst of our difficulties, too often we allow ourselves to
wave away self-control because life is already too difficult. For me, sometimes mental strength involves my mouth. There are moments when I
need the strength to open my mouth with wisdom for those who are
unable to speak up for themselves. But there are also times when I need
to swallow my pride, operate in self-control, and ask God for the strength
to keep my mouth shut. Not defend myself. Not justify myself. Not spout
off an opinion. Shut. My. Mouth. *Argh!*

Fortunately self-control is also a fruit of the Holy Spirit.[8] That means, because the Spirit lives in us, we have self-control—we just need to exercise it. I remember one time I came home from a challenging day. I'd had a conflict with someone at work and had navigated a tough situation with a friend. As I picked up my son from school, he said something with just enough disrespect to set me off. And over the top I went! Yes, he needed to be corrected, but I didn't practice the mental strength of self-control. I overreacted rather than responding appropriately to this specific situation. And I only created more trouble, more hurt, and more stress.

Emotions are an incredible gift, yet most of the time I find that rather than our managing them, they control us. We do so many things because we "feel" or "don't feel" like it. This can get us in serious trouble and will certainly prolong any storm, whereas building and toning that mental strength can prepare us for any trouble that comes our way.

GROWING OUR SPIRITUAL STRENGTH

Let's not forget about spiritual strength! We've been discussing this throughout the book, so I hope you're already in the process of building this type of strength. In talking about spiritual strength, the apostle Peter wrote that God has given us everything we need to live a life pleasing to Him. Then he challenged us:

> Don't lose a minute in building on what you've been given,
> complementing your basic faith with good character, spiritual
> understanding, alert discipline, passionate patience, reverent
> wonder, warm friendliness, and generous love, each dimension
> fitting into and developing the others. With these qualities active
> and growing in your lives, no grass will grow under your feet, no
> day will pass without its reward as you mature in your experience
> of our Master Jesus.[9]

I love this description of spiritual strength. It makes it less mystical and more practical. Spiritual strength comes from: *Alert discipline. Passionate patience. Reverent wonder. Warm friendliness.* In the middle of the storm, can you find your brave and work on building those? I love that it says to build wonder. In the middle of my year from hell, I found myself getting cynical and bitter. Regularly I had to discipline myself to see wonder in something. A baby. A sunset. The moon. Something. Anything.

How are you doing in the wonder department? How is your relationship with God? Is it real? Is it maturing? Are you letting His Spirit grow good character, spiritual understanding, passionate patience, and generous love in you? Are you reading your Bible? Do you spend time praying?

The apostle Paul wrote that we should "pray continually."[10] Is that merely some religious phrase, or can we actually pray continually? If I am going to be spiritually strong, then I must pray. I certainly have a daily time when I pray, but I also pray as I go about my day. When I am driving (with eyes open), in my heart before a hard conversation, or at the end of the day. And James even encouraged us to pray when we are happy or sick or when we make a mistake.[11]

The disciples watched Jesus for three years. They had seen Him praying in every circumstance and understood that He lived a life empowered by prayer. Perhaps that is why they asked Him, "Lord, teach us to pray."[12] Of all that they could have asked Him, they asked Him to teach them to *pray*. If we are going to be spiritually strong in the midst of our struggles, we must pray.

So do you hate me? I know it feels personal when someone tells you what to eat and when to sleep, to exercise, to read more, and to pray. I hope it felt less like nagging and more like someone coming alongside you to encourage you to build your physical, mental, and spiritual strength. I am doing the work right along with you.

Together we can do this. Together we can find our brave and get strong so we can make it through this storm.

The Other Side

Those who trust the LORD
will find new strength.

—Isaiah 40:31, CEV

Go as far as you can see. When you
get there, you can see farther.

—B. J. Marshall

D o you like movies? I do, but most of the time, before I go to the
theater, I ask people who have already seen the movie, "Does it end
well, or at the very least, does the end make sense?" I don't mind all the
ups and downs, emotional journeys, or scary adventures as long as the
ending makes sense!

Endings matter.

Did you see the TV series *Lost*? It was such an interesting show with
great characters, crazy adventures, a weird group of people called the
Others, mysterious smoke, hidden buildings, a secret code—and the
worst last episode ever! Seriously, so disappointing. I heard from someone
who worked on that show that it was because they never expected it to last
that long, so they didn't have a plan for a satisfying ending.

Well, unlike the writers of *Lost,* when God starts something He has the end in mind. It might be different from what you envisioned, and it will be better—ultimately—than what you can imagine! Because I like to know the ending, I am going to share one with you: "I know the thoughts that I think toward you, says the LORD, thoughts of peace and not of evil, to give you a future and a hope."[1]

This was written to the Jewish exiles in Babylon who had been forced by King Nebuchadnezzar to leave Jerusalem. They were living far from home and all that was familiar. It might have seemed as if all their hopes and dreams had been crushed. Maybe they wondered if God had forgotten them. In the midst of their fear, God assured them that He was thinking about them. How awesome that in the midst of our storm, in the midst of our pain, the God of the universe is thinking about us. He knows who we are and where we are.

Not only is He thinking of us, but also His thoughts toward us are good. His thoughts toward us are of peace. He has not turned away from us. He intends to give us a future filled with hope. Some versions say He will give us a "final outcome" or "expected end." This is good news. Obviously because God is eternal, our expected end includes heaven, but it also means there is an end to this season, an end to this storm. Yay! In the midst of the storm, sometimes we can focus on the big waves and forget that God is still on the throne. He is still God, and He has a future filled with hope for you and for me. We can find our brave in the middle of a storm when we remember this truth and allow it to shape our thoughts and attitudes into gratitude.

PRACTICING GRATITUDE

The storm was still raging and battering fiercely against Paul's ship. And he chose to do something that feels foreign to most people.

Paul expressed thanksgiving. Paul had just offered food to the sailors so they could regain their strength, and then he began to praise God. He knew that this storm was not the end of his story. He found his brave and encouraged the other sailors to find theirs by remembering that God was still God. The waves might be raging, but God had not forgotten them. They needed to raise their eyes from their surroundings and look up to God, who is bigger and greater and more powerful than anything that storm could throw at them. When Paul did that, he found it easy to offer thanksgiving.

He . . . gave thanks to God.
—Acts 27:35

Sometimes we can be too focused on survival (and surviving is good), but let's remember to keep our eyes on the God who calms the wind and the waves. Who has a plan for us—and it's good, bringing healing and peace with it. Who thinks good thoughts about us and has a promising future for us. Who has chosen us to share the good news with others and help them get to their shores as well. Isn't that great news to be thankful for?

God Is with Us

I have a few weaknesses. Well, actually more than a few. But one of them is that I tend to try to do too much in my own strength. As I mentioned in the previous chapter, it is important to do what we can to increase our strength so that we can endure the storm. But we can't forget that it is His strength that will see us through to the other side. Sometimes I try to figure out exactly how everything is going to turn out. Are you like that? That is actually not our job. Our job is to trust and obey God. Just like that song I sang growing up in Sunday school: "Trust and obey, for there's no other way to be happy in Jesus, but to trust and obey." I don't have to figure out how it will all work out. I can go ahead and fire myself from trying to run the universe—and choose to trust God.

After Moses died, Joshua became the leader of the children of Israel. Previously he had been Moses's assistant, and I'm sure he probably felt unqualified to fill Moses's shoes. After all, Moses had been an amazing leader. He had parted the Red Sea with just a staff; he had asked God for food, and manna appeared every day; he even talked to God face to face. Facing that kind of comparison, it would have been understandable if Joshua had been intimidated by his new role. That is why God reminded Joshua that He would be with him—just as He had been with Moses.[2] This reminder also let Joshua know that the reason Moses could do what he did was because God had been with him. Moses obeyed, and God made it happen.

God is saying to you and me, in whatever situation we face, that He is with us. We can trust Him. Often we find ourselves coming face to face with our own inability, face to face with our need for Him. And it is in those situations that our need for Him becomes clear.

As Joshua led the people into the Promised Land, I would imagine that he was nervous, especially as the first city to conquer was the seemingly unconquerable, walled city of Jericho. And God told the Israelites to attack it in an unconventional and seemingly crazy manner.

> In ancient warfare, such cities were either taken by assault or siege, surrounded until the people were starved into submission. Invaders might try to weaken the stone walls with fire or by tunneling, or they might simply heap up a mountain of earth to serve as a ramp. Each of these methods of assault took weeks or months, and the attacking force usually suffered heavy losses.[3]

But that wasn't the plan for Jericho. God simply told Joshua to have the people march silently around Jericho's walls for six days. On the seventh day, after seven marching circuits, the people were to shout down the walls. Shout.

If I were Joshua, I'd think, *Uh, this is weird. Got another plan, God?*

Though it seemed a crazy way to conquer a city, Joshua followed God's instructions to the letter. For six days, the people marched. On the seventh day, they marched around Jericho seven times, and that seventh time around, they whooped and hollered, yelled and roared. And the massive walls collapsed. Israel won an easy victory.

What was God doing? He was arranging the situation so only He would get the glory. No human got the credit for the wall fall. This victory was a gift from God. This is how God works: we find ourselves in positions where we are desperate for His power, and then He displays His greatness! It is in those circumstances that His name is praised.

If we are not only going to make it through the storms but also arrive stronger on the shore on the other side, we must remember that our God will never abandon us. We find our brave when we remember that He holds us in His hands.

I love these words of the prophet Isaiah:

Surely you know.
　　Surely you have heard.
The LORD is the God who lives forever,
　　who created all the world.
He does not become tired or need to rest.
　　No one can understand how great his wisdom is.
He gives strength to those who are tired
　　and more power to those who are weak.
Even children become tired and need to rest,
　　and young people trip and fall.

But the people who trust the LORD will become strong again.
They will rise up as an eagle in the sky;
    they will run and not need rest;
    they will walk and not become tired.[4]

Rising up like an eagle is such a beautiful and powerful illustration. My husband loves learning about eagles. Recently he told me a tale of a certain type of eagle that can, at one stage in his life, develop a wart-like growth on his beak. When this happens, this eagle's life changes. Normally, a healthy eagle can spot his prey from two miles away and, at one hundred miles per hour, swoop down on it with amazing precision. But now, the eagle with the growth dives for prey and misses. He slowly loses his accurate sense of perception and so cannot hunt effectively. He grows weary and loses his strength. When he lands, his balance is off and he stumbles to a stop.

With his skills diminishing, he seems to get confused and doubt his own abilities. The eagle actually begins to appear depressed, and soon he starts to lose his beautiful feathers. He retreats to the darkness of a cave, continuing to weaken.

Then something interesting happens. It is as though the eagle plans suicide. Either he wants to destroy himself or he realizes that he is about to die, so he decides he might as well do some flying. Perhaps he remembers what it was to soar above the clouds, to be the king of the air. He steps out of the cave, looks toward heaven, and begins to flap his tired wings. He lifts off and heads straight up. He goes higher and higher. He rises above the clouds and keeps going.

As he continues to gain altitude, the atmospheric pressure changes and the growth on his beak bursts. When it bursts, he is immediately energized with fresh power and strength. His equilibrium returns. His depth perception comes back. He is once again himself. He can hunt with precision and strengthen himself.

This story about the eagle may or may not be true, but the Bible is true. Isaiah told us that if we would trust God and remember that He is on the throne, then we too would rise like the eagle. When we put our eyes and our hope on the God of the universe, we are strengthened. Those things that are trying to destroy us are themselves destroyed as we look up. In the midst of the storm, keep looking up. It is easy to get freaked out—or at least distracted by the waves—but never forget who is taking care of you. Find your brave by keeping your eyes on your God.

Worship Strengthens Us Too

Have you read the Bible lately? Not just reflected on how important Scripture is, but actually read God's Word? Have you taken time to worship God—more than just on Sunday morning at church?

Some say, "I know how important worship is." But what I'm asking is, "Have you worshiped Him?" Worship has nothing to do with singing in key (good thing for some of us!). It isn't even necessarily singing. It certainly includes singing, but really it is just declaring Who. He. Is. He is our God, our Protector, our Comforter, our Healer, our Peace, our Provider. When we worship God, we can see our problem from His perspective, and suddenly our huge storm looks manageable!

Many times this past year I took my phone with its worship playlists out to my backyard. I turned up the music loudly and sang and shouted. I did what Paul did during his storm. I shouted thanks to God for His presence, His love, and His faithfulness. I did not know how everything was going to turn out; I just knew I needed His presence.

Our church services start with worship. Our amazing team and band lead the congregation in corporate worship. It is a time when we can express gratitude to the God who loves us. I love this time. Still, over the years, there have been moments when I did not want to go to church (not a good thing for a pastor). I did not want the eyes of people on me. I wanted to be alone, and yet as a leader, I knew my job was to lead people to focus on Christ. Which meant that I went to the front row of our church and worshiped with everything in me. The more I worshiped, sometimes with tears streaming down my face, the freer I felt. The more I worshiped, the more confident I was that God would see me through whatever challenge I was in. I can worry, or I can worship. I can't do both.

Acts 16 tells us that Roman soldiers beat Paul and his fellow missionary Silas because of their faith. They flogged the men to within an inch of their lives. Bleeding and in serious pain, Paul and Silas found themselves in prison. Somehow, in this horror, they began to praise God. They began to sing to Him.

I don't think this was a conscious plan. Paul didn't tell Silas, "Look, let's sing and praise God, and then He'll send an earthquake to deliver us." No. I imagine that in a cracked, hurting voice, Paul asked, "Silas, how are you doing?" I can hear Silas moan, and then Paul say, "You know, Silas, the only thing that will improve this place is His presence. We need the presence of God."

They reminded themselves who was on the throne. And as they praised Him and expressed their gratitude to the King of kings, He entered the scene. He always does.

As a side note: it says the other prisoners listened to Paul and Silas's worship. Those men who were also in pain probably wanted what Paul and Silas had. We know the jailer did. It is the same in our lives. Hurting people are all around us, watching, listening, and needing what we have. Do we invite God's presence to abide with us? Do we praise Him in the midst of our prison cells?

In one scene in the movie *Selma*, Martin Luther King Jr. was in jail with his friend Ralph Abernathy. King was talking about the obstacles and the danger in which he had placed the people around him. He was worried and tired, and he wondered if it was worth their fight for the right to vote when so many of his people were illiterate and impoverished. As King shared his concerns, Abernathy began to quote from the gospel of Matthew: "Look at the birds of the air: they neither sow nor reap nor gather into barns, and yet your heavenly Father feeds them. Are you not of more value than they?" Ralph didn't know the answer to King's questions, so he just reminded him they could trust God with the journey.

You will not get all of your questions answered, but can you still rest in the knowledge that God has not left you? Maybe you have just gotten divorced and are wondering if you will ever love again. Can you trust God that it is not the end of your journey? That He will lead you. Maybe you just filed for bankruptcy and have no idea what the future holds. Will you begin to declare, even softly, that "He will never leave me or forsake me"?

TRUSTING GOD WITH THIS MOMENT

One day Jesus had spent hours and hours teaching and healing people. The day had been full and Jesus must have been tired and ready for a rest. That evening, He and the disciples got into their boat to cross to the other side of the sea. As soon as He was settled in, He went to sleep.

The other side lay at the end of a six-mile journey. Several of the disciples were veteran fishermen, having fished this lake for years. They had grown up on its banks, its shore had been their boyhood playground, and they knew its every curve, current, and mood. These men were handy with oars and sails. The Lord was in safe hands when He boarded that boat. This was their realm and He could leave the sailing to them.[5] Or so they believed.

As they were crossing, a storm of hurricane proportions arose unexpectedly. Of course the disciples were taken by surprise. As fishermen, they knew what the sky and water looked like before a storm. They never would have left the shore if they thought a squall was coming. So they were surprised to find the waves beating against their boat, threatening to overturn and sink their vessel, and they were afraid.

And yet in the midst of the storm, Jesus slept!

The disciples were drenched to the skin and at the mercy of the raging winds. It grew so terrifying that the disciples woke Jesus. But not just a little poke and shoulder shake. The word *awoke* in this story is the same word that is often used when referring to rising from the dead. That is a powerful awakening! They jerked him up and said, "Hey, don't you care about us? We are perishing!"

Jesus barely took time to wipe the sleep out of His eyes before He took care of the situation. He rebuked the wind and the waves. He said, "Hush now! Be still (muzzled)! And the wind ceased (sank to rest as if exhausted by its beating) and there was [immediately] a great calm (a perfect peacefulness)."[6] One word from Him, and the winds and waves would do His will.

Then He turned to His buddies, His disciples, and asked them why they were afraid. He asked them why they had no faith. He was not talking about faith in the abstract—or faith in a vacuum. Faith always has an object. It is linked to something or someone. We exercise faith in the pilot when we board a plane. We have faith in the bank when we hand over our deposit.

Jesus asked His disciples why they had no faith—in *Him*. Jesus challenged them: "Why did you fear? Why don't you have any faith? Why could you not *trust* Me—*Me*?"

He asks the same question of you and me. The presence of Jesus on board does not necessarily guarantee a smooth passage. What we are promised is His presence in the storm. He is in our boat, and He is at rest. He wasn't sleeping because He didn't care; He was sleeping because this was no big deal. Not in the big picture. The same God who called you to the other side is not panicked in the middle. You might be. I have been. But He is not. God's intention for you and me hasn't changed. We have been promised a future filled with hope. This storm does not change that. He is Lord of the whole journey, and He is Lord of this moment.

Our greatest temptation in a storm is to put our trust in something other than God. Rather than losing our heads and thinking we just need another joint, drink, job, french fry, or man to see us through, let's remember who is on the throne and in our boat.

When a storm hits, God can do one of two things: calm the storm, or calm you and me in the midst of it. We find our brave because He is in charge. Never forget that!

He Is with You—No Matter What the Circumstance

Over and over, Scripture reminds us: our God can get us through any situation. Psalm 107 in The Message paraphrase is such an encouraging read. It's a little long, so rather than quoting here, I'll let you go ahead and open your Bible (or go to Biblegateway.com, if you don't have The Message).

I love the picture the whole chapter presents. The writer describes how some people found themselves in a desert: hungry, thirsty, with no place to call home. But then God stepped in, satisfied the hunger and thirst, and led them home.

Some found themselves in a prison of depression, emotionally suffering. Then He saved them; He brought them out of their gloom and darkness.

Some had even turned away from God; they were in misery and alone. But His love healed them, and they were saved.

Some were in a stormy sea, the waves crashing around them. They lost their courage. They did not know what do to. But then He calmed the storm, stilled the waves, and guided them to port.

I don't know what kind of situation you are in. If it is the barren, dry, desert kind, He will satisfy your thirst. Maybe you feel hopeless in your marriage. Perhaps you are choking in the chains of depression. Maybe your financial situation is desperate. Maybe you are overwhelmed at work. Maybe you are confused about a decision you are facing. Maybe your heart has been broken. Maybe you feel all alone. Remember who is on the throne. Don't let fear cause you to take your eyes off your King. Because He is with you. And He is for you.

The one thing that is certain to change in life is circumstances, which is why the Bible tells us to trust not what we can see but rather what we can't.[7] The circumstance you are in right now will not last forever, so don't put your faith or your focus on the power of the storm but in Him who will see you through it. I am not saying that is easy, because the storm can be so loud. Maybe the expression of our faith in God, our worship, should be louder? I'm sure as Paul began to thank God on that ship, he was shouting it over the winds to remind himself that God is bigger than that storm was.

What was encouraging to me over these last few challenging, scary, annoying, painful years was the knowledge that the same God who started the work in me is the One who will finish it.[8] *He will finish it.* He knows the beginning and He knows the end. Regardless of what we might feel right now, our greatest days are ahead, because with every new circumstance, God is shaping us into the image of Christ. We are a work in progress, and God will finish what He started. He is the God who parted the Red Sea, opened blind eyes, and raised the dead. I can certainly trust Him to finish what He started in me. My job is just to trust and obey.

The more we trust, the braver we become. It was because of Joseph's obedience that he rose to the rank he was given in Pharaoh's court, and thousands were spared from starvation. Joshua had to be obedient and enter the Promised Land and conquer the people living there. Esther did not have to figure out how God was going to rescue her people, she was just obedient and a nation was saved. Jesus, trusting His Father, was obedient as He went to the cross and humanity was saved. God will finish what He starts.

I don't pretend to know what you are going through—I can't imagine. Still, I am confident that God created you for a purpose, that He loves you, that He has begun a good work in you, and He will be faithful to complete it.

Have you begun to lose your focus in the storm? Does the storm feel larger than life? Do your problems feel overwhelming?

Friend, I want to encourage you. How big is your problem in light of who God is? Consider buildings, the really tall ones. (I am going somewhere with this. Promise.) If you saw a photo of a skyscraper with a human next to it, you might think, *That building is really big.*

Well, the building isn't really that big when you compare it to a mountain. According to LiveScience.com, the tallest building in the world is Burj Khalifa in Dubai and the tallest mountain from base to summit is Mauna Kea in Hawaii. It would take twelve of Burj Khalifa stacked on top of each other to be as tall as Mauna Kea in Hawaii. If you were to do that, you'd realize, *Wow, mountains are big, aren't they?*

Well, they aren't really that big when you compare them to our planet. When you see a satellite photo of earth taken from outer space, the highest mountains look like specks of sand. You might think, *Our planet is really big, isn't it?*

Well, it isn't really if you compare it to, say, the sun. It would take more than one million of our Planet Earth to match the size of the sun. *That's amazing. The sun is really big, isn't it?*

Well, it isn't really that big if you compare it to some of the other stars in the galaxy. One of the stars in the galaxy is so enormous that it would take fifty million of our sun to match its size. *Now that is a very big star.*

Well, not really, if you consider that this is one star in a galaxy in which there are billions of stars. *All righty, then. The galaxy is massive, isn't it?*

Well, not really, because there are billions of galaxies. There are enough galaxies out there that every human being could have at least fourteen of them—fourteen galaxies apiece. *Whew!*

So the universe must be pretty big, then. And to think that our God created it just by saying, "Let there be stars and galaxies."

Now consider your problem in light of our Creator and all He has created. Is anything we face really too big for God? Your storm might be huge. But no one wants you delivered from this storm more than your heavenly Father.

God saved Paul and the ship's crew from certain death because He had a purpose for them. And it was on the other side of the storm. In the same way, He has plans for your life beyond the storm. We can trust Him. We can focus on Him and His presence with us. We can worship Him. We can thank Him. And in all those things, we find our brave.

It might feel as though He's asleep in our boat, but when we call His name, Jesus responds.

When You Make Your Own Storm

The marvelous richness of human experience
would lose something of rewarding joy if
there were no limitations to overcome.

—Helen Keller

There are two kinds of people: those who
say to God, "Thy will be done," and those to
whom God says, "All right, then, have it your
way."

—C. S. Lewis

The movie *Twister* was certainly entertaining. Maybe because I don't live in the tornado zone, I could watch it and not take any of it personally. (The flying cows were weird, though.) Don't get me started about the movie *San Andreas,* a film about a magnitude 9 earthquake—basically the complete computer-generated-imagery destruction of California. A little too close to home. What was interesting to me about *Twister* was that the scientists had all of this incredible equipment they used to chase storms—not avoid them, but seek them out. They risked their lives looking for tornadoes. They hoped to figure out what caused them so they could predict them . . . but still, they were hunting down storms. We may not be chasing twisters, but some of us bring storms on ourselves because of the choices we make.

Can I be a spiritual mom to you for a moment? Or a big sister? Or at least a friend? I have made plenty of bad choices, some of which I have written about in this book, so I know what it is to stir up trouble with bad decisions.

Does one of the following describe a situation you are familiar with?

- Maybe you are in a financial storm because you have consistently spent more than you earn. It won't take too many months of this spending pattern to create a storm.
- Maybe you had sex with someone, and it turns out he had an STD. Now you do too.
- Maybe you had a few drinks before you left for home. Only you didn't make it home. A police officer stopped you, and now you are the proud owner of a DUI ticket and all that involves. Or perhaps you had an accident while under the influence, broke your legs, and hurt someone else too.
- Maybe while your husband was out of town, you casually went out to dinner with someone from the office. Now you find yourself attracted to him and wonder if you ever were really in love with your husband. This new man seems so much more exciting. Or maybe you simply stopped investing the necessary energy into building your relation-ship with your husband. Either way, marriage storm.
- Maybe you were so lonely that you married the first guy who asked. Never mind that he didn't know God, still prefers to party with his single guy friends, and can't keep a job. Now you find yourself in a storm because you said "I do" when you should've said "I don't."

- Maybe you did so many drugs that you lost your family, or maybe you have smoked for years and now have emphysema or lung cancer.
- Maybe junk food has been your staple for years, and now you are significantly overweight and your health has taken a hit.
- Maybe like me, you cheated on a test, got caught, and now you have a big fat F in a class.
- Maybe like me, you let an offense settle into bitterness, and now you have to deal with the much harder job of pulling up that root.

All of these are painful situations to be in. And so many of them could have been avoided had we not gone down paths that we really should not have traveled.

IGNORING WISE ADVICE

Before the voyage even began, the apostle Paul knew the trip was doomed. Remember they were traveling during the off-season for sailing, which inevitably meant rough weather. So Paul warned the officer in command that there was trouble ahead if they continued with this trip. And the officer made a choice that too many of us also make when we choose not to listen to the wisdom of others who are looking out for our best interest.

The officer did not listen and neither did the captain, and since you have read the book so far, you know that it was not a good decision. It was indeed too late in the season to sail, and they encountered a storm that nearly cost their lives. This captain made a decision that not only landed him in a serious, life-threatening storm but also put everyone else on board at risk. The storms we stir up in our own lives will always affect others as well as ourselves.

How often do we ignore the warnings, knowing in our heart that the choice we're about to make isn't the best or wisest? Just a few months ago, as I write this, a cargo ship went directly into the path of a hurricane. The ship was headed from Florida to Puerto Rico and never made it. The ship took on water and then sank, killing all on board. And what was worse was that the crew's family claimed that the crew knew the ship might not have been in the best shape to make that kind of trek but pushed through anyway, despite the warnings. Devastating.

We had lost a lot of time. The weather was becoming dangerous for sea travel because it was so late in the fall, and Paul spoke to the ship's officers about it. "Men," he said, "I believe there is trouble ahead if we go on—shipwreck, loss of cargo, and danger to our lives as well." But the officer in charge of the prisoners listened more to the ship's captain and the owner than to Paul.

—Acts 27:9–11, NLT

The lesson, of course, is that we need to listen to wise counsel and warnings. But coulda-shoulda-woulda doesn't help when we pushed right through, made a bad decision, and are now smack-dab in the middle of our own storm. Is there hope even then? Yes, as we see from Paul's story. But it will take a little work to get to the other side.

You Are Not the Captain of Your Own Ship

If we are going to get out of the storms we have created, we must give up control and realize we are not the captain of our ship. Too often we cling to the ship's wheel as though we can force life circumstances to fix themselves, even while we're the ones who messed things up. But being a follower of Jesus means surrendering our way for His.

Maybe you are looking at your life right now and thinking, *This is a mess.* I've had that thought a few times. Okay, more than a few. Are you wondering how you got here?

Remember the story of the prodigal son that Jesus told in Luke 15? I briefly referred to it in an earlier chapter but want to unpack it more here. The younger son found himself in a terrible situation—a pigpen, to be exact—and he asked himself the same question, "How did I get here?" When I read his story, I realize there were steps he took that led him to the pigpen. He might not have realized the ultimate consequences, but he did take the steps. We might have more in common with him than we thought.

Like hurricanes, we can easily move from a Category 1 to a Category 5. Here is what those look like in the storms we cause.

STORM CATEGORY 1: FEELING ENTITLED

The Millennials—those born between 1981 and 2001—have been called the most entitled generation. I don't know if this is true or not, but there are dozens of books written about how to hire them, talk to them, and work with them. According to most of these books, Millennials were raised by hovering helicopter parents, rarely disciplined, and were given a trophy even if they never showed up for soccer practice. Employers become frustrated by some Millennial employees who want a promotion after working two years and who want the life they see older people have—only they want it now. They feel they deserve it, that they're entitled to all the benefits and privileges, without necessarily working for it.

To be fair, this attitude of entitlement spans all generations. Who among us hasn't at times bought into the "I deserve it because it makes me happy and I'm worth it" mentality? The parable of the prodigal son makes clear this attitude is not unique to Millennials.

The prodigal son's first mistake: he began to feel entitled. He believed the world owed him something. As a young man, he wanted to leave home and strike out on his own. Not an unusual desire for a young man—but he wanted to use his inheritance as a springboard. Like the captain on Paul's ship, he decided to make his own plans. Maybe home life was getting too hard. Maybe he was tired of doing what others wanted or expected him to do, or maybe he was sick of hearing his older brother complaining that he didn't do his fair share. Who knows? Basically he said, "I want what's mine, and I want it now!" Dr. Kenneth Bailey, a Bible scholar who has lived and taught in the Middle East for more than forty years, suggests that the younger son, by wanting his share of the estate right then, was in essence saying to his dad, "I wish you were dead."

He goes on to say, "In response to such a request, Middle Easterners would expect a father to explode with anger, slapping the son in the face with an open backhand. Yet in the parable, the father unexpectedly grants his son's request." The text says that the father divided his living. Dr. Kenneth Bailey explains that "living" comes from the Greek word *bios,* which means "life." So "the text should read, 'And he divided his *life* between his sons,' which more accurately captures the depth of the father's pain."[1]

The money would one day have indeed been the son's. He was supposed to receive his inheritance at the right time—which would have been at his father's death. Until then, he was supposed to help his father, faithfully building and supporting another man's vision. Then he would have been entrusted with his own.

Instead, he wanted it right then. Why? He felt he was entitled to it. This is the first step toward creating a storm: feeling as if we have a right to something.

Perhaps you feel that your boss owes you a bigger salary, so you grumble at work. Or you know you do put in more hours and effort than your coworker, so you deserve that better office. I am not saying you can't ask for a raise or the better office, if you think it is appropriate. But the "I deserve" attitude will only create a storm in your workplace.

Maybe you are a phenomenal keyboard player in your church band. You think you are so good that the church leadership ought to put your name in the bulletin or set the piano center stage. You are headed for a storm. There will always be people around to feed your ego, saying, "You are so good, Miss Piano. You deserve your own spotlight!"

Whatever it is that makes you believe you deserve something rather than being grateful for God's gifts to you (see our previous chapter), be on the lookout for a potential storm. Entitlement is the first step to a storm of your own making.

STORM CATEGORY 2: BECOMING SELF-INDULGENT

The second step the prodigal took on his way to creating a storm—and the second step you and I take on our journeys toward trouble—is that he began to be incredibly self-indulgent. Self-indulgence is thinking about *me . . . me . . . me.* This is when we do anything to satisfy every desire we have. Perhaps at times we can all be a little self-indulgent, when our ego or desire shouts to be taken care of. Maybe because the prodigal was the younger son, he wanted to feel important, so he left home and spent his money on whatever made him feel good. This guy was out blowing his inheritance on fancy clothes, fancy women, and a fancy house—all to satisfy a desire. When we begin to feel that people owe us and then try to satisfy that feeling in a self-indulgent way, we are headed for rough waters.

If you are married and begin to think, *I deserve sex whenever I want* or *I deserve to be understood, and I am not getting it here, so I'll look elsewhere,* you are headed for trouble. Trying to fulfill our desires through extramarital flings—or eating too much or spending money we shouldn't—is a disastrous choice.

A self-indulgent person has lost sight of her true identity. She has forgotten she is a child of the King, created with a purpose. And the self-indulgent woman is usually the last to notice it. It is pretty obvious, though, to those around her: the self-indulgent person doesn't care about anyone but herself.

Self-indulgent people do not consider how their actions might affect others; they are focused on their own needs and wants. They are too busy taking time to satisfy their desires, regardless of the ultimate cost to themselves or to anyone else. My need to be right, to win an argument, has often led me to keep pushing until there is a crack in my marriage. Is being right really the highest goal? Or for another woman, her need for excitement or companionship might lead her to an affair, but the consequences to her children will be an unstable home.

Self-indulgence provides momentary pleasure, comfort, and significance, but over time, we find ourselves without purpose, empty, and alone. It is easy to look at those self-indulgent people "over there." How about looking into your own heart? And I will look into mine. Life throws enough storms our way, so we should really try to avoid the ones we cause ourselves!

Storm Category 3: Abandoning Accountability

The third thing the prodigal son did to create a storm was to leave the people who cared for him. Maybe he was fed up with the judgment of his older brother, but when he departed from his childhood home, he left those who loved and supported him—and he abandoned accountability. In his immaturity, he left wisdom, perhaps because he felt it was limiting. After all, if we are self-indulgently entitled, the last thing we want to hear is a friend or family member tell us that we are acting self-indulgently entitled and that our actions don't please God. Proverbs puts it this way: "He who willfully separates and estranges himself [from God and man] seeks his own desire and pretext to break out against all wise and sound judgment."[2]

God did not design you and me to do life alone, apart from loving, wise counsel. When we separate ourselves not only from God but also from the people He has placed in our lives, we're in trouble. We will grow and flourish *only* when we are connected to each other. Paul's ship captain shows us that truth clearly!

Maybe you feel so badly about choices you've made that shame drives you away. Don't let it! You will only face an even greater storm. Perhaps someone in church hurt your feelings, and rather than getting over the offense, you chose to leave the very people God sent to help you grow and heal. God set up a safeguard system for us, and it's called One Another. It is not only those people in AA or Celebrate Recovery who need accountability—it is all of us. I understand that sometimes it seems as if it would be easier to get away from the people who know our business, but in the end, isolation will not serve us well.

In my own life, there have been many times in the middle of the storm where picking up the phone or meeting a friend for dinner and sharing the truth (the whole truth, so help me God) was difficult. I would have preferred to isolate and hide and pretend as though I had it all together. You know what I have discovered? *None* of us has it all together, so we might as well be in our mess with friends, rather than stuck at home alone.

Storm Category 4: Choosing Bad Company

After the prodigal son had spent all his money, there was a famine in the land. A famine is a season of scarcity, deprivation, and shortage. We have all endured periods of lack—in finances, peace, vision, or hope. Famines are scary and seem endless.

In his need, the young man began to work for a citizen of that country. Having separated himself from God and the people who loved him, he joined himself to someone who didn't know God or anything about following Him. We know this because he owned pigs—animals the Jews believed were unclean. His employer sent the prodigal to feed his herd. To a Jew, this would have been the most disgusting job possible. (Actually, I think it's pretty disgusting too.)

This fourth step toward a storm of our own making comes when we join ourselves with someone who doesn't know God or His Word, and so can't help us get to shore. I am not saying that we shouldn't spend time with people who are not believers. Jesus spent time with all sorts of people. The difference is that Jesus was a blessing to the people He met; He changed their lives. When we are running from God and choose the company of people who don't serve Him, rarely are we a blessing to them. All we do is bring our storm into their lives and vice versa.

The more time we spend with people who do not know God, or who are not committed to following the ways of God, allowing them into our inner circles, we begin to pick up their habits. We do unclean things. The shame that follows is terrible. The unworthiness we feel is awful. When we're in a storm, we might settle for things we never would otherwise. We settle for pig slop until even it begins to look good.

Sometimes the wrong people are simply the wrong voices. We might let social media influence us way more than it should. We compare our life with someone else's Instagram feed, and then we feel bad. Of course we do. No one puts their bad days on their feed! As pastor Steven Furtick has noted, "This is one of the main reasons we struggle with insecurity: we're comparing our behind-the-scenes with everybody else's highlight reel."[3] And perhaps on Facebook we engage in commenting, and then commenting on someone's comments, and then find ourselves feeling like we are in the mud. Be careful whose voice you allow to speak into your soul.

We all have legitimate needs, which include significance, peace, intimacy, companionship, and love. How we meet these needs is what is crucial. I have known women whose desperate desire to be married (a legitimate need) caused them to begin relationships with men who were not good for them. Some of the men were even abusive. Now of course, God can turn anything around, and He is with us always, but their decisions just simply made their lives harder.

I know people who have destroyed their lives and families with drugs and alcohol, only to now be living with people who continue to pull them down. I have seen others who have tried to satisfy the pain in their hearts by spending money they don't have, and they are now in serious debt. Some have even linked themselves to not-so-nice people to get loans. Again, God is right there with them in this mess that started with the decision to meet a legitimate need in the wrong way. But each storm category of our own making leads us to another until we feel as if our boat is sinking.

The good news is that we know from Scripture that the prodigal son didn't stay with the pigs. He found the way home. So can we. We can find our way home to God's grace, and He will help us out of the storm.

So what does the prodigal reveal about how we can find a way through, and beyond, the storm?

LESSON 1: COME TO YOUR SENSES

The prodigal son was ashamed as he found himself, the son of a very wealthy man, envying pigs because at least they had food. He finally came to his senses. The King James Version of the Bible says "he came to himself." Maybe he started to remember who he really was. We are never our true selves when we separate ourselves from God. The son realized that even the servants in his father's house had a better life than he did. (Well, duh!) He knew there was something else—something better. He remembered his father and his old life, not just to reminisce but also to do something about it.

If we look around and find ourselves in the pigpen—a storm of our own making—we need to stir ourselves up to take action. We can't settle for what we have. If we realize that we are not living the life God has promised, which is an abundant, confetti-throwing, parade-riding life, then we must come to our senses. Changing the course of our ship and sailing for smoother waters begins when we remember who we are. Jesus paid a great price for us to live lives of purpose. His sacrifice on the cross removes the shame of our past and enables us to move forward in grace toward a future filled with hope.

LESSON 2: GET HUMBLE

After we come to our senses, the next thing we have to do to get out of our self-made storm is to humble ourselves. The prodigal son realized that he was going to have to do this before his father. He prepared himself to say, "Father, I blew it. I know I am not even worthy to be called your son, so I will come back as a servant."

Humbling ourselves and admitting fault or failure is not so easy for most of us. The Bible challenges us to humble ourselves. People already know we make mistakes; they want to know if we have the integrity to admit them. Cheating on that test in college led me into a storm. I felt entitled to a better grade, so I cheated to get it. This led to embarrassment before professors and students. I had a choice. I could deny it or get defensive—or I could humble myself. I chose to humbly acknowledge my mistake before a panel of my peers. Not a fun day. But the first step toward restitution at school.

I have made mistakes at work, with friends, and in my marriage. Sometimes I have gotten impatient with a coworker thinking something should have been done differently. My impatience never helps the situation, and often damages the work relationship. I have learned to be quick with "I'm sorry." It goes a long way toward restoration. While I would certainly like to think that all of the challenges Philip and I have in our marriage are his fault, the reality is that I have said and done things that have not communicated respect. When he feels disrespected, he withdraws and then we have a mess. I have a choice: I can defend my position (which I always think is right), or I can say, "I'm sorry," and mean it. Not just throwing out the words, but *meaning* them. I don't know about you, but my first instinct is to get defensive. Defend my position. It never helps. Humbling myself and apologizing has always proven to be an important first step out of the mess I created. It won't cleanse everything and stop the storm; it won't make a wronged friend trust you again; it is just the first step.

So if you find yourself in a storm of your own making, you can start escaping it by coming to your senses, then find your brave by humbling yourself. Admit you were wrong. Say you're sorry. Admit responsibility for hurting the people around you. Avoid getting defensive, so that you can put the pigpen behind you and move forward into the abundant life God wants for you.

LESSON 3: REPENT

The next thing the prodigal son did to escape his storm was to repent, simply to turn and go in the opposite direction. He had to move; otherwise, he would have stayed in that pigsty, feeling humiliated. Repentance —saying "I'm sorry" *and* changing course—involves making decisions that take you in the right direction.

If you have made financial decisions that hurt your family, saying "I'm sorry" isn't enough. You must begin to adjust how you handle money. If your lifestyle has produced a weak and unhealthy body, feeling sorry about it is not enough. You must choose to take care of your body— and that choice must involve practical steps. If you have hurt others with your choices, you will have to take responsibility and make changes to earn back trust and move forward in those relationships. Be brave. You can do this.

Repentance for the prodigal son meant that he began walking in a new direction. And when he took those steps to get out of his mess, he found his father waiting for him. While the son was still a distance away from home, the father saw him, had compassion on him, and ran to him.[4] God is like that. He is looking for us as we turn back to Him. The Bible says not only did the father race to greet him, but he "threw his arms around him and kissed him."[5] Dr. Bailey tells us,

> In the Middle East, it was considered a humiliation for a middle-aged man to run and to lift his robe exposing his legs as he ran. Yet the father ran. The Greek word used is *dramon,* a term used for a footrace in a stadium. Further, the father *repeatedly* kissed the son. The Greek word *katephilesen* means kissed again and again.[6]

He is the God of the second and third and fourth chances!

The father didn't say, "I told you so." He gave his son a robe, sandals, and a ring. He loved. He couldn't give him back the years, though. That is the sad part. We will never get back the time we waste in our self-inflicted storm. The word *prodigal* actually means "wasteful," and the young man certainly was wasteful with money but also, more importantly, with time. God will take all of our failures and work it out for His good and our good, but we will never get back those hours, days, or years. Let us resolve, then, to make the most of the days, weeks, and months we have on earth. This story really shouldn't be called the story of the prodigal son, because he is not the hero. The hero is the father, who represents our God. His posture toward us is always one of open arms. Even when we are the ones who get ourselves into trouble, He always welcomes us home.

BRAVERY IN ACTION

Dee is part of our church family, and a young woman I have had the privilege of knowing and loving. When Dee came to our church, her life was a wreck—she was in a serious self-induced storm. She had been addicted to hard drugs for a lifetime, had been in and out of rehab, and was traumatized from the years she spent in the sex industry. During her childhood, Dee experienced physical, mental, and sexual abuse. She also suffered the loss of many family members. She was afraid to get too close to people in fear that they would either abandon her or that God would take them. Dee believed that God was punishing her by killing the people she loved. This young woman was positive that she was beyond God's reach, that she had wasted half of her life, that God wasn't interested in her, and that she belonged to the dark side.

Can you imagine the courage it took for Dee to come to a church? When she did, she met some incredibly brave friends who saw beyond her mess and introduced her to the Savior. She took the first step and humbled herself, acknowledging her need for God. She admitted that her way was not the way. Dee said yes to Jesus and began her journey home. I don't know about you, but when I first said yes to God, all of the issues in my life didn't just go away—I had to do a little work. So did our beloved Dee.

She was at what I call Door Number 1: a saved mess. She was so very loved by her God and on her way to heaven . . . but still a mess! You see, God doesn't love us more the longer we follow Him. He loves us unconditionally—even while we reject or fear Him. He loves us when we make bad choices that result in a storm, and He loves us when we make good choices. His love never changes.

Once we say yes to Him, we are on the journey of working out our salvation.[7] We can park ourselves at Door Number 1 and never move, if that's what we choose. If we do that, however, we will probably die before our time—and God doesn't need us dead. If He did, we would all be in heaven, singing with the angels. He needs us alive and well on the planet, fulfilling the purpose for which He created us. He needs us to live. He needed Dee to live. He had a purpose for her to fulfill.

So God began to talk to Dee. As she felt God's love through her friends, He started to speak to her about her life and He began to reveal Himself as more than her Savior. He was her Healer as well. Dee attended our GodChicks conference for the first time in 2008. My friend Nancy Alcorn was speaking at a session, sharing miracle stories from Mercy Ministries and imparting hope to the women. As Dee sat under the teaching, she felt the Holy Spirit convict her. *Is God trying to give me a rule to follow? Is serving God all about the rules? No! God loves me and needs me to live. Drugs kill.* Jesus did a miracle that day, and she was completely set free from meth. Miracles are not always instantaneous, but her desire for meth was completely removed that day. She even went to her car, grabbed all her drug paraphernalia, and brought it to the altar to Nancy and me. (That was the first time that had happened!) She repented—she began to go in a new and better direction.

Her friends, Nancy, and I, and loudest of all, God, applauded her, saying, "Way to go, honey!" (Well, that's how He talks to me.) He let her rest in that victory. But soon He began to talk to her about the next step on her journey. Remember, it is not about the rules; it's about living to fulfill destiny.

God began to challenge her sexual addiction. God is not trying to take away Dee's fun. He wants her to live. He wants her body and heart to be whole and healthy. The truth is, it is a toss-up what will kill you first: sleeping around or doing drugs. Our church has buried people who caught diseases from having sex with partners they shouldn't have. And don't believe the world when it tells you that condoms can keep you from getting sexually transmitted diseases—they can't.

As Dee began to understand her value was not in her sexuality, she began to open her heart and trust more. She started to release controlling, manipulative behaviors, and the truth of the Word of God began to counter the lies of the Enemy. She read her Bible, replaced the wrong voices with the right ones, and began to learn about sexual purity. At the time, this seemed like such a hard door to walk through. She eventually yielded to God's way. After all, her way had brought only pain. Dee finally came to believe she had value and a purpose and overcame her sexual addiction.

And again, God celebrates her choice. He doesn't love her any more now than He did before she said yes to Him; she just has a better chance of living long enough to fulfill His purpose for her. Dee has gone on to overcome depression, and through God's grace, she has forgiven herself of her past. Dee travels and speaks, sharing her story. She leads a survivor-led support group for other women who are beginning to take their first steps out of addiction. Dee is a walking miracle, and at every door, God has been faithful to receive her, and so has the body of Christ. The road hasn't been easy, but because of what Jesus has done for her, because of God's great love, Dee continues walking through every door and welcoming others to join her on the journey.

If you are in a storm of your own making, God's arms are open to you. Come home to His grace and rest assured that, one step at a time, He will lead you out of this storm. He can heal your heart, your mind, and your body.

The Shore

She believed she could, so she did.

—R. S. Grey

We made it, friend. We found our brave as we navigated the storm. God is faithful and He did what He promised. The winds have died down, the sun is out and shining brightly, and the waves are calmed. And life looks promising again. Yay!

And God proved faithful to Paul and the ship's crew too.

Everyone made
it to shore safely.

—Acts 27:44, MSG

Paul and the others made it to shore by hanging on to boards and swimming for all they were worth. Though they hadn't reached their intended destination, they knew God had been faithful—the shore is land, after all! Now everything was going to be great, right?

Just When You Thought You'd Made It . . .

According to Acts 28, Paul and the sailors were catching their breath, drying off, and resting by a fire the natives provided. All of a sudden, a snake crawled out of the pieces of wood in the fire and bit Paul's hand. As if he hadn't suffered *enough*? First of all, he was a prisoner, then he was on a ship for weeks enduring a dark, horrible storm, then the ship crashed, he had to swim to shore, and then, a snake had the nerve to bite him! Have you ever felt like that? Just when you think all the bad stuff that's going to happen is over—*wham,* here comes another hit.

Paul handled the snakebite with his usual cool style. He just flicked off the snake. Of course, it freaked out everyone watching. But not Paul. They thought he would surely die. But Paul trusted God with this situation, just as he had trusted Him with the storm. He was not going to let a snake do to him what a storm and a shipwreck couldn't. We need a little of that tenacity.

It seems as if storms just keep on coming, don't they? Although I hope yours won't be a snakebite, I can assure you it will be something. The good news is that you will be stronger and more equipped for the next one. You will be more virtuous—just as the Proverbs 31 woman was. Remember her? The Bible says she was prepared for winter.[1] This passage might have meant a literal winter. (It is really tough to prepare for winter here in Los Angeles . . . hmm, which bathing suit should I wear? The blue or the black one? I am sorry. #NotSorry.) But it is definitely speaking of dark times. She, this incredible woman—you—is prepared for any storm that comes. Because you have found your brave, the next storm won't knock you out!

Regardless of what's coming, don't forget that the same power that raised Christ from the dead is inside you.[2] Because that is true, you can walk in peace and confidence and really find your brave. Live today knowing that.

REACHING THE SHORE IS ABOUT
MORE THAN WE THINK IT IS

Paul and his shipmates had landed on the island of Malta, which was not their original destination. What? They were supposed to go to Rome! I'm sure neither Paul nor the sailors had a plan that included Malta . . . but God did. This is the God who works all things together "for the good of those who love him."[3] People on the island needed to have an encounter with the living God, and Paul was just the guy to bring it to them. Getting through the storm had a higher purpose. Not only did those sailors find their brave, but they met others on the island that needed to find their brave too.

After my cancer diagnosis, I was introduced to a world of people who had never crossed my path before. I learned about many alternative cancer treatments and used quite a few of them; however, the one traditional treatment I underwent was radiation. This meant I had to show up to the cancer treatment center every day for seven weeks. I was angry at the fact that I had the disease, and I loathed even the thought of radiation, so obviously, I did not want to be in that waiting room.

I showed up on day one, folded my arms, and stared at the floor, waiting for my name to be called. Then I went to the treatment room, had the treatment, and left. On day two, I showed up in the waiting room angry, folded my arms, and stared at the floor, waiting for my name to be called. Then I went to the treatment room, had the treatment, and left. On day three, I showed up in the waiting room angry, folded my arms, and stared at the floor, waiting for my name to be called. Then I went to the treatment room, had the treatment, and left. On day four, I showed up in the waiting room angry, folded my arms, and stared at the floor, waiting for my name to be called. Are you getting the picture here? While I was in that waiting room on day four, I felt the Spirit of God whisper to me, *Holly, look up.*

"No."

I did not want to see those people.

But eventually I did look up, and I saw people in far worse condition than I was. I saw people with both legs amputated and people with brain tumors who were having radiation done to their head. I overheard conversations, and for some this was their last chance. I looked into the eyes of everyone in that room, and in many of them I saw fear, hopelessness, and loneliness.

I knew what God was asking of me. He wanted me, as His daughter, to be His hands and feet in this place. He was asking me not only to find my brave, but also to bring the hope that I had in Christ to this roomful of people who desperately needed it too. And can I say that I did not want to? After all, I was dealing with cancer myself. Everyone would have understood if I just focused on my own issues. And yet I knew what God was asking of me.

So on day five when I showed up to that room, I brought cookies for everyone—of course they were the disgusting healthy ones that no one really wanted, but I passed them around anyway. I started conversations and got phone numbers. I handed out some books and prayed for people. For the next seven weeks *these* people became *my* people. This was not the place I wanted to be. This was my Malta. It wasn't in the original plan, and yet I knew, just as Paul knew, that God could work all things together for good for those who love Him.

There are people on your shore as well, who need the life and presence of God that is in you. They need to find their brave. God is not looking down at you and me in our storms and feeling sorry for us. No! He is looking way down the road He has called us to travel. He sees a whole bunch of people He needs us to touch with His love. After all, we are His hands. So maybe you feel a bit weak and overwhelmed by all you've endured (we've all been there), or maybe you think the storm has knocked you off course. Nope. You are in His hands. If you open your eyes, you will see lots of people around you—they are waiting for you to get up.

You have made it through a tremendous storm, and other women out there need to know how you did it. Perhaps you single-handedly raised your children into responsible adults (a miracle for any of us). I guarantee you there are women in your circle of influence who need to know what you did and how you did it. You may have overcome tremendous marital storms, managed to stay married for fifty years, and still love that man. We need to know what you know. The same is true if you have lived through tremendous abuse and found the path of healing, or if you have overcome serious debt. Your past can help give someone else a future. You can help someone get through a storm simply by sharing what you know—and someone out there needs your help.

As a woman like you who is doing her best to ride out the storms of life, let me say this: We have a responsibility as His daughters to get through them. We actually don't have the luxury of camping out in the valleys or letting the storms sink us. We are supposed to be examples to those who may not know Him; we are to show them how to live victorious lives—not perfect ones—just committed to the parade, regardless of the circumstances.

Each of us is responsible for the generation coming behind us. Christianity is a relay race, and there are legends of faith who have gone before us.[4] They have navigated their storms, and now it is our turn to find our brave and then help others find theirs.

Paul challenged us: be strengthened, or perfected, completed, and made what you ought to be.[5] Storms have a way of doing this. God is making my marriage what it ought to be because Philip and I are riding out our storms. God is developing me into a stronger leader because I am learning to humble myself and forgive. I have friendships today that God is beautifying because we didn't give up on each other when things got uncomfortable. My faith is taking its ordained shape because I believe in God and His plans. I just keep on breathing, believing, and daring, and my faith grows stronger.

When my marriage was at its stormiest and I was complaining to

God about Philip, I was sure God felt sorry for me. I was sure He could see just how hard I had it. There were moments during this time when I feared I had married the wrong person, and Philip was convinced he had made the same mistake. Most of us have thought that at one time or another! Had I messed up my destiny?

I finally realized that God wasn't feeling sorry for me at all. But He was ever present, ever ready, and ever willing to get me through the storm. I'm sure God was waiting for me to get to the shore, because I would arrive stronger and more mature, but also because He had other struggling couples He needed me to help. He was right. Philip and I have helped thousands through their storms because we understand what being in a storm is like. We always think our storm is supreme and that we can't possibly get through it, but there are people attached to our obedience. There are always others we are to help once we reach the shore.

After I navigated cancer, I have talked to thousands of women as they battle cancer themselves. After dealing with leadership challenges, I have helped hundreds of other pastors handle similar challenges. Parenting is rewarding and challenging, and after I navigated some challenges with my children, I have been privileged to help others. There will be others for you to help—just on the other side of this storm. You will find them everywhere on your shore.

I know girls who have struggled with eating disorders or self-harm. I find that most eventually want to help other young women, to keep them from doing what they did. Yes. That is the biblical response.

Remember, not only is Jesus in the storm with you, but He is also looking at where He has called you to go.

So What Will You Choose?

The God we serve is a good God. Still, we live in a world where good and evil exist together. When challenges and storms come our way, we get to choose how we react. God did not create us as puppets; we do have a say.

Will we let the storm refine us or define us? Will we commit to trusting God through it or will we sink? The decision is entirely ours. The storms we navigate will change us. We can get bitter, or we can be made stronger. We can close our heart to people or open it wide, believing that there are people we need to help. We can look back and wish for something different, or we can look ahead and trust that God will meet us there.

The trial, if we let it, can bring out the best in us. As the diamond is revealed only after the piece of coal has been under pressure, the treasure in us can be exposed only when the storm hits. And those around us will benefit as we do.

In the seventeenth century, John Bunyan wrote *The Pilgrim's Progress* from a prison cell. One of the bestselling books of all time came from that author's serious storm. Martin Luther King Jr. wrote "Letter from Birmingham Jail" while he was in captivity. During World War II, Dietrich Bonhoeffer's *Letters and Papers from Prison* emerged from his sojourn behind bars. And of course, Paul continued to travel and share the good news of the gospel to anyone and everyone. In the midst of incredible challenges and extreme adversity, these individuals found their brave . . . and treasure appeared.

In the storms I have navigated, I have learned patience, because I have discovered that the journey is the destination. How I do life is important. And the truth is, if I do life His way, then the destination will be incredible—far beyond what I could imagine or think!

Recently as wave after wave crashed against my life, from cancer to betrayal to identity theft, from marriage woes to friend wounds, I was able to hang on by getting rid of excess baggage, dropping anchors, building up my strength, embracing His presence, worshiping in the hope of what is to come, and reminding myself daily that God is on the throne. To the best of my ability, I did and am doing all that I have shared with you in this book.

I wish battles and storms just came one at a time—or really, never at all!—but they don't. They often come all at once. Make the decision that the third or fourth or tenth storm won't take you out. You found your brave once; you can do it again. And along the way, watch for the magnificent shore, and for the people God has prepared for *you* to help find their brave.

Scriptures to Speak over Your Situation

As we talked about, the Word of God is powerful. It is the weapon God has given us to fight our battles, and it can be used to refocus our mind to the truth. Here are some Scriptures for you to write in a journal, meditate on, or speak out loud over your situation.[1] Let His Word be your strength in the middle of whatever storm you find yourself.

Exodus 14:14: "The LORD himself will fight for you. Just stay calm."

Exodus 15:2: "The LORD is my strength and my song; he has given me victory. This is my God, and I will praise him—my father's God, and I will exalt him!"

Deuteronomy 31:6: "Be strong. Take courage. Don't be intimidated. Don't give them a second thought because GOD, your God, is striding ahead of you. He's right there with you. He won't let you down; he won't leave you."[2]

Deuteronomy 31:8: "Do not be afraid or discouraged, for the LORD will personally go ahead of you. He will be with you; he will neither fail you nor abandon you."

Joshua 1:9: "This is my command—be strong and courageous! Do not be afraid or discouraged. For the LORD your God is with you wherever you go."

---

1 Chronicles 16:11: "Search for the LORD and for his strength; continually seek him."

Psalm 9:9: "The LORD is a shelter for the oppressed, a refuge in times of trouble."

Psalm 16:11: "You will show me the way of life, granting me the joy of your presence and the pleasures of living with you forever."

Psalm 18:32–34: "God arms me with strength, and he makes my way perfect. He makes me as surefooted as a deer, enabling me to stand on mountain heights. He trains my hands for battle; he strengthens my arm to draw a bronze bow."

Psalm 23:4: "Even when I walk through the darkest valley, I will not be afraid, for you are close beside me. Your rod and your staff protect and comfort me."

Psalm 27:1: "The LORD is my light and my salvation—so why should I be afraid? The LORD is my fortress, protecting me from danger, so why should I tremble?"

Psalm 34:7: "The angel of the LORD is a guard; he surrounds and defends all who fear him."

Psalm 50:15: "Call on me when you are in trouble, and I will rescue you, and you will give me glory."

Psalm 55:22: "Give your burdens to the LORD, and he will take care of you. He will not permit the godly to slip and fall."

Psalm 61:3: "You are my safe refuge, a fortress where my enemies cannot reach me."

Isaiah 40:28–31: "Have you never heard? Have you never understood? The LORD is the everlasting God, the Creator of all the earth. He never grows weak or weary. No one can measure the depths of his understanding. He gives power to the weak and strength to the powerless. Even youths will become weak and tired, and young men will fall in exhaustion. But those who trust in the LORD will find new strength. They will soar high on wings like eagles. They will run and not grow weary. They will walk and not faint."

Isaiah 41:10: "Don't be afraid, for I am with you. Don't be discouraged, for I am your God. I will strengthen you and help you. I will hold you up with my victorious right hand."

Isaiah 41:13: "I hold you by your right hand—I, the LORD your God. And I say to you, 'Don't be afraid. I am here to help you.' "

Isaiah 43:2: "When you go through deep waters, I will be with you. When you go through rivers of difficulty, you will not drown. When you walk through the fire of oppression, you will not be burned up; the flames will not consume you."

Lamentations 3:22–23: "The faithful love of the LORD never ends! His mercies never cease. Great is his faithfulness; his mercies begin afresh each morning."

Matthew 11:28–29: "Jesus said, 'Come to me, all of you who are weary and carry heavy burdens, and I will give you rest. Take my yoke upon you. Let me teach you, because I am humble and gentle at heart, and you will find rest for your souls.' "

John 14:27: "I am leaving you with a gift—peace of mind and heart. And the peace I give is a gift the world cannot give. So don't be troubled or afraid."

1 Corinthians 10:13: "The temptations in your life are no different from what others experience. And God is faithful. He will not allow the temptation to be more than you can stand. When you are tempted, he will show you a way out so that you can endure."

2 Corinthians 5:17: "Anyone who belongs to Christ has become a new person. The old life is gone; a new life has begun!"

Philippians 4:6–7: "Don't worry about anything; instead, pray about everything. Tell God what you need, and thank him for all he has done. Then you will experience God's peace, which exceeds anything we can understand. His peace will guard your hearts and minds as you live in Christ Jesus."

Philippians 4:13: "I can do everything through Christ, who gives me strength."

2 Peter 1:3–4: "By his divine power, God has given us everything we need for living a godly life. We have received all of this by coming to know him, the one who called us to himself by means of his marvelous glory and excellence. And because of his glory and excellence, he has given us great and precious promises. These are the promises that enable you to share his divine nature and escape the world's corruption caused by human desires."

Questions for Personal Reflection and Group Discussion

Chapter 1: Rising in the Darkness

1. What is the most recent earthquake you've experienced? In which areas of your life were you left scrambling to find your footing?

2. Holly explains that the word *virtuous* in Proverbs 31 is translated from the Hebrew word *chayil*, which "has to do with might, strength, and valor." How does it feel to know that God is calling you, as a woman, to be strong and powerful—a "force on the earth"?

3. What does it look like to be a woman who "rises" when trouble and heartache come (Proverbs 31:15, ESV)?

Chapter 2: Brace Yourself

1. When have you found that your thoughts affected the outcome of a situation for either good or bad?

2. What do you know for certain about who God is right now? What Scriptures are you using to brace your mind so that the truth is more real than the facts of your situation?

3. Do you find it easy or difficult to ask someone else for help? Why do you think that is? King Solomon wrote, "Two are better than one" (Ecclesiastes 4:9). What friend are you holding on to as you ride out this storm? And because there are others who need you, what friend are you helping through her storm?

Chapter 3: Let It Go

1. Just for fun: on the last trip you took, did you pack anything you didn't use? If so, what was it?

2. What hurts—related to friends, family, finances, school—are you carrying around now? What lies are you believing about who you are, or who God is, that cause you to hold on to the baggage in your life?

3. Holly suggests four pieces of baggage that we need to throw overboard if we're to weather the storms in our lives: past hurts, unmet expectations, fear, and insecurities. As you consider each of those burdens, which one seems the heaviest in your life right now? What would it look like on a practical level to throw it overboard today?

Chapter 4: Keep the Main Thing the Main Thing

1. Consider a decision, either small or large, that you face today. In what ways can you keep God's kingdom a priority in your decision-making process?

2. What role do relationships—with God and others—play in finding your brave?

3. Identify a goal you've set for yourself and describe how you've gotten sidetracked. What distractions are cluttering your mind, schedule, and priorities right now? What would help you get back to focusing on the main thing?

Chapter 5: Get Your Hopes Up

1. Sometimes we use the word *hope* to mean "wishful thinking." What is the true meaning of the word *hope*? Why do you think the author of Hebrews referred to hope as an anchor (6:19)?

2. In Romans 5:3–4 we read, "Suffering produces perseverance; perseverance, character; and character, hope." When have you seen suffering lead to hope in your life or in the life of someone you know?

Chapter 6: Courage Is a Decision

1. What is the difference between *feeling brave* and *believing in God as your bravery*?

2. Romans 8:28 tells us that God "causes everything to work together for the good of those who love God and are called according to his purpose for them" (NLT). How does this truth help you find your brave today?

Chapter 7: Anchored

1. When you face difficult circumstances, what is the most common way for you to try to numb your pain? How would a deeper awareness of your true identity and purpose help you anchor yourself in God instead?
2. Describe the relationship between worship and contentment. Are you attending church, or are you actually planted in the house of God? What is the difference?
3. Following Holly's model, write your own declaration of freedom.
4. How do you want to be remembered? Are you living your life in a way that will cause you to be remembered the way you want? Explain your answer.

Chapter 8: Don't Quit!

1. Describe something in your life that you are tempted to quit. What truth about God helps you keep going?
2. What role model—either someone in history or someone you know personally—inspires you to live with determination to follow through on what you started?
3. Why do you think God asks us to do impossible things?

Chapter 9: Stronger

1. How do you view your body and God's desire for you to care for your body? In what ways do you care for yourself through physical exercise, healthy eating, and rest?
2. In general, do you feel that you control your emotions or that they control you? Why?

3. Describe a recent time when you experienced wonder. Why do you think wonder keeps us from growing cynical?

Chapter 10: The Other Side

1. Holly writes, "The presence of Jesus on board does not necessarily guarantee a smooth passage. What we are promised is His presence in the storm. . . . The same God who called you to the other side is not panicked in the middle." How does this description compare with your own perspective in the midst of challenging circumstances? Picture Jesus asleep in the boat in the middle of a current storm in your life. How does His peacefulness shape your response?

2. How would you experience storms in your life differently if you truly believed God has a future hope for you?

Chapter 11: When You Make Your Own Storm

1. When have you done something you regret because you wanted to control a situation?

2. Are you in the middle of a storm of your own making? What would it look like to come to your senses, get humble, and repent? How would those actions help you find your brave?

Chapter 12: The Shore

1. Holly writes, "We can look back and wish for something different, or we can look ahead and trust that God will meet us there." How could you show, through your thoughts and actions, that you are looking ahead to the shore in the midst of a storm today?

2. After reading *Find Your Brave,* in what ways do you feel more equipped for whatever storm may come next in your life?

3. What encouragement could you offer today to help someone else in your life find her brave?

Acknowledgments

Although my name is on the cover as author, I don't believe any book—and certainly not one of mine—is really the work of one person. For more than thirty years, I have been in the house of God listening to and learning from wonderful men and women of God. Over the years I have heard countless teachings, read thousands of books, had conversations with hundreds of people, and spent hours and hours getting to know my God. It is through all of these influences that these words have been penned. I have tried to give credit where credit is due, so if I somehow missed you, please forgive me and know that I am grateful.

Fifteen years ago I wrote a book using a similar outline to this one. And I think about twelve people bought it. Honestly, I had no business writing the book then. It was a good outline, and as a teacher, I know a good outline. But I hadn't navigated enough storms to be able to write it. I hadn't yet earned the scars. Now I have.

Thank you, Rachel Corbucci, for your help in keeping all the pieces of my life together. You are a legend and I am grateful!

Thank you, Ashley, for giving the book the first work out. Your encouragement and help were invaluable!

Thank you, Ginger Kolbaba, for your insights, intelligence, humor, and help in whipping this book into shape. This book is better because your hands were on it. I still think you probably threw a shoe or two at your computer!

Thank you, Laura Barker, for believing in me and for your commitment to get this message out.

Thank you, Esther, for believing that the message of this book will help people. You are a gift to me! I look forward to lots more adventures in the years ahead!

I love my church, Oasis Church. Together we have been on a journey. I owe much of who I am to the incredible people of the Oasis.

Thank you, Philip. So much of you is in me and in this book. I love you. Thank you for the words and the stories. I am stronger and better because of your love and belief in me, and I consider it an honor to weather the storms of life with you.

And most important, thank You, Jesus, for Your presence in every storm. My life is not my own; use it as You so desire.

Notes

Chapter 1: Rising in the Darkness
1. 1 Peter 4:12
2. John 16:33
3. *Strong's Hebrew and Chaldee Dictionary of the Old Testament* H2428, www.bibletools.org/index.cfm/fuseaction/Lexicon.show /ID/H2428/chayil.htm.
4. Proverbs 31:15, ESV
5. Judges 4
6. Esther 5–7
7. *The Apologetics Study Bible for Students,* ed. Sean McDowell (Nashville, TN: B&H, 2010), 1194.

Chapter 2: Brace Yourself
1. 1 Peter 1:13, CEV
2. Romans 10:17
3. John 14:9, CEV
4. Romans 12:2
5. Proverbs 31:10, AMP
6. Jeremiah 29:11
7. I do need to clarify something. If you are in an abusive, violent marriage, get out and please get help. You don't have to do this alone.
8. Malachi 3:10
9. Philippians 4:19
10. Ecclesiastes 4:9–11

11. 1 Corinthians 12
12. Proverbs 18:1, NKJV.

Chapter 3: Let It Go

1. Matthew Henry, *Matthew Henry's Commentary on the Whole Bible,* version 1.5 (Altamonte Springs, FL: OakTree Software Inc.).
2. Matthew 5:44
3. Sophie Henshaw, "How to Cope with Disappointment," *Psych Central* (blog), October 20, 2013, http://psychcentral.com/blog /archives/2013/10/20/how-to-cope-with-disappointment.
4. Hebrews 13:5
5. James 1:2–4
6. Romans 5:3–5
7. Psalm 37:4
8. 2 Timothy 1:7, NKJV
9. 1 Samuel 17:48
10. Numbers 13:30, NKJV
11. Hebrews 10:35
12. Proverbs 31:10, AMP
13. 1 Corinthians 12
14. Romans 12:2
15. Psalm 81:6; 1 Peter 5:7
16. Matthew 11:30

Chapter 4: Keep the Main Thing the Main Thing

1. Stephen R. Covey, *First Things First* (New York: Simon and Schuster, 1995), 75.
2. Matthew 6:33
3. 1 Timothy 1:5, AMP
4. Mark 12:28, 30–31
5. Luke 15:11–32
6. Hebrews 11:6

Chapter 5: Get Your Hopes Up

1. John 14:2
2. Acts 27:22–26
3. Romans 12:15
4. John 16:33
5. Lamentations 3:19–24, MSG, emphasis added
6. Psalm 56:8
7. 1 Samuel 30:1–8
8. Psalm 103:1
9. Mark Bittman, "Everyone Eats There," *New York Times Magazine,* October 10, 2012, www.nytimes.com/2012/10/14/magazine /californias-central-valley-land-of-a-billion-vegetables.html?_r=0.
10. John 4:10
11. Romans 5:3–5
12. John 16:33, AMPC
13. 2 Corinthians 2:14, MSG
14. Holly Wagner, *When It Pours, He Reigns* (Nashville: Thomas Nelson, 2004), 22.

Chapter 6: Courage Is a Decision

1. Joshua 1:2, NLT
2. A sermon I heard a few years ago by Scott Scruggs emphasized the point that everyday courage is what God is asking of us.
3. Luke 22:42
4. Mimi Haddad, "Brave-Hearted Women," *Charisma,* January 31, 2004, www.charismamag.com/site-archives/24-uncategorised /9843-brave-hearted-women.
5. James E. Kiefer, "Gladys Aylward: Missionary to China," http:// justus.anglican.org/resources/bio/73.html.
6. Habakkuk 3:19, AMPC
7. Joshua 1:9, MSG
8. Philippians 3:20

9. Ephesians 2:6
10. 2 Corinthians 5:20
11. Romans 8:28–29, NLT
12. Ephesians 2:10, NLT
13. 2 Corinthians 4:17, NKJV
14. 2 Corinthians 11; Acts 28:3–6
15. Philippians 1:20
16. Romans 8:28
17. Romans 8:27, MSG
18. 2 Corinthians 3:18

Chapter 7: Anchored

1. Dana Bartholomew, "Northridge Earthquake: 1994 Quake Still Fresh in Los Angeles Minds After 20 Years," *Los Angeles Daily News,* January 11, 2014, www.dailynews.com/general-news /20140111/northridge-earthquake-1994-disaster-still-fresh-in -los-angeles-minds-after-20-years.
2. Robert Schuller, *Tough Times Never Last, but Tough People Do* (New York: Bantam, 1984), 179–80.
3. *Tyndale Commentary,* ed. Donald J. Wiseman, version 1.5 (Altamonte Springs, FL: OakTree Software Inc.).
4. US Declaration of Independence, July 4, 1776.
5. Romans 8:37
6. Daniel 4:17, MSG
7. Luke 10:19
8. 2 Corinthians 3:17
9. Isaiah 1:18
10. Esther 4:14
11. Matthew 13:21
12. Lydia Brownback, *Contentment* (Wheaton, IL: Crossway, 2008), 9.

13. Matthew 6:25
14. John Phillips, *The John Phillips Commentary Series,* version 1.1 (Altamonte Springs, FL: OakTree Software Inc.).
15. *Tyndale Commentary.*
16. 1 Thessalonians 5:18
17. Philippians 4:12–14, MSG
18. Philippians 4:8–9, MSG
19. 1 Timothy 3:15
20. Bobbie Houston, *Heaven Is in This House* (San Antonio, TX: Maximized Leadership, 2002), 26–27.
21. Psalm 92:13–14

Chapter 8: Don't Quit!

1. "Biography of Susan B. Anthony," National Susan B. Anthony Museum and House, 2013, https://susanbanthonyhouse.org /her-story/biography.php.
2. B. L. McGinnity, J. Seymour-Ford, and K. J. Andries, "Anne Sullivan," Perkins School for the Blind, www.perkins.org/about /history/anne-sullivan.
3. "Naomi's Journey Home," DoNotDepart.com, March 10, 2011, http://donotdepart.com/naomis-journey-home.
4. Ruth 1:18
5. James 1:2–4
6. Mark 6:45
7. Mark 6:48
8. Mark 6:48
9. 2 Timothy 4:7
10. Acts 14:19–20
11. Hebrews 12:1–2, MSG
12. Judges 8:4
13. Isaiah 28:6

Chapter 9: Stronger

1. Proverbs 24:10
2. Proverbs 31:17, AMPC
3. 1 Corinthians 6:18–20
4. 1 Corinthians 9:24–27, AMPC
5. Dr. Myron Wentz, *Invisible Miracles: The Revolution in Cellular Nutrition* (Scottsdale, AZ: Medicis, 2002), 8.
6. *The Surgeon General's Report on Nutrition and Health,* US Department of Health and Human Services (Public Health Service), 1994, 1.
7. Ira Dreyfuss, "Exercise Found as Effective as Antidepressant Zoloft," *Los Angeles Times,* October 1, 2000, http://articles.latimes.com/2000/oct/01/news/mn-29539.
8. Galatians 5:22–23
9. 2 Peter 1:5–8, MSG
10. 1 Thessalonians 5:17
11. James 5:13–15
12. Luke 11:1

Chapter 10: The Other Side

1. Jeremiah 29:11, NKJV
2. Joshua 1:1–9
3. "What Should We Learn from the Walls of Jericho Falling Down?," GotQuestions.org, www.gotquestions.org/walls-of-Jericho.html.
4. Isaiah 40:28–31, NCV
5. John Phillips, *The John Phillips Commentary Series,* version 1.1 (Altamonte Springs, FL: OakTree Software Inc.).
6. Mark 4:38–39, AMPC
7. Hebrews 11:1
8. Philippians 1:6

Chapter 11: When You Make Your Own Storm

1. Kenneth Bailey, "Meaning of Prodigal Son Parable," www
   .eprodigals.com/The-Prodigal-Son/The-Prodigal-Son.html.
2. Proverbs 18:1, AMPC
3. Steven Furtick, *Crash the Chatterbox* (Colorado Springs, CO:
   Multnomah, 2014), 27.
4. Luke 15:20
5. Luke 15:20
6. Bailey, "Meaning of Prodigal Son Parable."
7. Philippians 2:12

Chapter 12: The Shore

1. Proverbs 31:21, NLT
2. Romans 8:11
3. Romans 8:28
4. Hebrews 11
5. 2 Corinthians 13:9–12, AMPC

Scriptures to Speak over Your Situation

1. Unless otherwise indicated, all Scripture quotations in this section
   are taken from the New Living Translation.
2. Deuteronomy 31:6, MSG

About the Author

Holly Wagner's life is full and busy—just the way she likes it! Like most women, she wears many hats: wife, mom, pastor, teacher, author, and cancer survivor. She grew up in Venezuela, Indonesia, and England, and eventually moved to Los Angeles, where she worked as an actress in films and television for more than ten years.

Today she and her husband, Philip, are lead pastors of Oasis Church, a growing, relevant, multicultural, multigenerational church they started thirty years ago in Los Angeles. She and Philip have taught many relationship seminars around the world and are committed to healthy marriages, especially their own! They love spending time with their two young adult children, Jordan and Paris.

Holly is passionate about seeing women become who God has designed them to become and about seeing every generation of women extend a helping hand to the younger generations. Through the women's ministry of Oasis and GodChicks, Holly seeks to blow the lid off the boxes that women have sometimes put themselves in and encourages women to be the amazing, world-changing champions they were made to be.

She has written several books, using her humorous yet challenging style to encourage readers. Her books include: *GodChicks,* which examines the many facets of being a woman of God; *Daily Steps for GodChicks,* a ninety-day devotional written during her breast cancer treatment; *Warrior Chicks,* which uses Holly's own life experiences to deliver witty, yet poignant, principles for facing the battles of life; *Love Works,* which she cowrote with her husband, Philip, and which offers practical help for dating and building a marriage. Her most recent devotional, *GodChicks Awakened,* is a daily challenge for all of us to awaken to our purpose.

Holly has been featured on many TV shows, including *Life Today* with James and Betty Robison, Dick Clark's *The Other Half, Berman and Berman,* TBN's *Praise the Lord,* JCTV, *The 700 Club,* and *The View.* Holly speaks at churches and conferences all over the world, and she loves living out the adventure God has given her!

———————————

Please visit Holly's website at SheRises.com.